Invitation to Philosophy

SECOND EDITION

INVITATION SERIES

Invitation to Philosophy

SECOND EDITION

Martin Hollis

Copyright © Martin Hollis 1985, 1997

First published 1985
Reprinted 1986, 1988, 1990, 1991, 1992, 1993,
1994, 1995, 1997
Second edition published 1997
Reprinted 1998

Blackwell Publishers Ltd
108 Cowley Road
Oxford OX4 1JF, UK

Blackwell Publishers Inc
350 Main Street
Malden, Massachusetts 02148, USA

British Library Cataloguing in Publication Data
A CIP catalogue record for this book is available from the British Library

Library of Congress Cataloging in Publication Data
Hollis, Martin.
    Invitation to philosophy / Martin Hollis.
        p.   cm. -- (Invitation series)
    Originally published: Oxford, UK ; New York, NY, USA : Blackwell,
1985.
    Includes bibliographical references and index.
    ISBN 0-631-20664-7 (alk. paper)
    1. Philosophy--Introductions.   I. Title.   II. Series.
BD21.H642   1997
100--dc21   97-7778
                                                                              CIP

Typeset by Katerprint Co. Ltd., Oxford
Printed and bound in Great Britain by
MPG Books Ltd, Bodmin, Cornwall

This book is printed on acid-free paper

For Simon and Matthew

Contents

Preface to the Second Edition

The aim of an Invitation, as I see it, is to convey the magic of a subject, rather than offer a current guide. That means less revision than an Introduction would need and changes to the first edition, although many, are mostly intended to make the text clearer and sharper. But new sentences and paragraphs will be found throughout and chapter 8 has acquired a section on Justice and Morality, where the Sensible Knave from Hume's *Enquiries* has been called in to make trouble for the idea that the demands of justice ensue from the mutual advantages of fair play.

As before, the book owes more than I can try to mention to my teachers, colleagues and students, who have fanned my philosophical curiosity since my own student days. I remain especially grateful to Adam Morton and Bernard Williams, whose acute and detailed comments on the original version led to many improvements, and to A.J. Ayer and Geoffrey Warnock for their welcome encouragement. Vivid memories of Ayer's skill as a tutor are a continuing inspiration. Nick Bunnin has been of great help in revising the Further Reading, and Jerry Goodenough has kindly revised the index for this new edition. Thanks are again due to the staff at Blackwell, in particular to Kim Pickin who steered the original edition through the press most helpfully and to Steve Smith who suggested this second edition. Simon Hollis, then a schoolboy, drew the picture of the Vanishing Philosopher in chapter 1.

The author and publisher gratefully acknowledge permission from Penguin Books Ltd to quote from H.D.P. Lee's translation of Plato's *Republic*, Penguin Classics, 2nd edn (revised), 1974, pp. 317 and 319–20.

1

Wonder, Paradox
and Vision

Is there conscious life elsewhere in the universe? That is an old question, asked for changing reasons. Lately it has become a scientific one, exciting because science just might be able to answer it. We have set foot on the moon and fired probes at the planets. We have radio-telescopes and computers to extend our puny reach. That hardly puts us nearer proving the negative – that nowhere in the infinite universe is there conscious life – but it starts to raise the chances of finding positive signs. The scientist's mixture of knowledge, ignorance and curiosity can go to work on the technical challenge.

The philosopher's curiosity has a different focus. Pause and think about the question itself. It is a little like asking whether there is gold under the polar ice, but only a little – we know gold when we find it. If a space probe flashed home pictures of blue Venusians waving cheerily, that would be like finding gold. But 'conscious life' embraces all sorts of other possibilities and, on reflection, we do not know where the limits might lie. Even in earthly biology it shades off into organisms which are not conscious; and work on artificial intelligence in computing holds out prospects of conscious systems which are not exactly living. As science fiction reminds us, there is nothing inherently special about our own head, two eyes, thirty feet of digestive tract and opposible thumbs. Somewhere between biology and computing there is an unmapped field which we do not care to prejudge. But scientific ignorance is only one reason why we are unsure what 'conscious life' embraces.

Questions have a purpose and this one is older than the technical curiosity of recent science. One enduring purpose of it has been to understand how human consciousness fits into the larger cosmos or order of things. Wonder at an unknown cosmos is as old as the sight of the stars from the mouth of the cave – wonder about what there is and how it moves and why the gods have ordered it so. Out of that wonder comes a puzzle about consciousness itself and a sense of an inner cosmos in uneasy relation to the cosmos outside. Human beings carry a world within them, different from the everyday world of the senses and imperfectly continuous with it. So, up to a point at least, do animals. They too are sentient, ingenious, purposive and organize a communal life. Perhaps they even dream. Yet they do not record the past in song and do not spy death coming nor wonder what lies beyond death. This is a profound difference. It may in the end be only a large one of degree, rather than one showing a difference in kind. But meanwhile it is marked by our human awareness of contrast between inner and outer worlds, a sense of self apart from experience, which is very hard to pin down.

Since long ago, then, mankind has tried to understand nature for reasons other than making life easier and more convenient. There has also been the challenge of our own human nature. We stand somehow at the juncture of inner and outer worlds, creatures of both body and spirit, subject to laws of nature yet making our own way. We are both part of the order of nature and separate from it; and the cosmos we glimpse is also a cosmos which we impose after our own manner of understanding. These are old perplexities (posed here in a way which later chapters will query) and they have long led thinkers to wonder if they are unique to ourselves. Is there conscious life, like ours, elsewhere in the universe?

It is worth stressing that the question is truly a practical one. By noting that it has now become one about the reach of technology, I may have seemed to contrast modern practicalities with ancient speculations. But there is nothing more practical than trying to discover how to live and, hence, how the universe is constructed. How we should live has much to do with what changes could in fact be engineered. That depends on what is essential to human nature and what is an accident of place and time. For example, humans have all sorts of desires, some making for a peaceful life together and others for strife and enmity. We are prone to love and sympathy and also to envy, hatred and malice. Some variety in the mixture is due to place and time; compare, for instance, the honour code of old Japan with the individualism of modern market economies or the aggressive impulses of classical Spartans with the peaceable sentiments of Quakers. Some desires are as enduring as maternal instinct and others as fleeting as the latest craze. It would be a very practical matter to know which were essential, either because we cannot remove them or because we would cease to be human if we did, and which could be set aside in a suitable environment. This is another reason to wonder whether there is conscious life elsewhere. Even speculation makes us define what we are assuming about the fixed and the variable components of human nature.

There is a difference between 'practical' in the sense of technically feasible and 'practical' in the sense of making a difference to how we live. It is practical in the latter sense to ask whether there is a God. But it is not practical in the former sense, and I do not wish to confuse them. My point is that questions about conscious life do not separate cleanly into the two senses. On the one hand, if we are going to build radio-telescopes to look for it, we need to decide what we are looking for. On the other, local information about the nature of consciousness is so elusive that fresh and perhaps disconcerting data might help us understand what we have already. By analogy, experiments with embryos in test tubes can disturb both our beliefs about the development of cells and our beliefs about the nature of persons. Theorizing (or the making of sense out of experience) involves both information and understanding, with no easy separation to be made between scientific and moral understanding. Later in this book I shall distinguish between knowing more and knowing better but this opening chapter is about the wonder and curiosity which inspire philosophy. They are not the peculiarity of peculiar beings called 'philosophers'. They are the motive of every thinking person's search for an order which makes scientific and moral sense.

That is why I picked an opening question, where theorizing brings the technical and the moral together.

Is there conscious life elsewhere in the universe? There is a question of fact here, one which would be settled, if we happened to find beings just like us beyond Alpha Centauri. But it is, at best, an imprecise question, since we are very unsure how unlike us something could be and still count as conscious life. Some of the imprecision could be removed by defining the terms 'conscious' and 'life' exactly. But this is not just a matter of defining them as we please, since it needs to be possible that discoveries in space will increase our understanding of conscious life. Part of the imprecision reflects our puzzlement about the nature of consciousness. Yet it is a curious puzzlement seeing that we live among conscious beings and have had many centuries to study ourselves. Hence, there is another sort of question involved, not wholly one of fact, nor of words but, obscurely as yet, of how to think. It is this kind of question, born in wonder but probing for order in matters of fact, which I shall pick out as typical of philosophy. Readers who have got this far will sense what I am after, since they will have been drawn to the book by their own philosophical curiosity. But an intuitive sense will not be enough for later chapters and I shall now draw a contrast between the *closed* and *open* questions, which prompt the search for knowledge or, to strike a rather different note, wisdom.

Closed Questions

Are there little blue people on Venus? That is a closed question, since it is clear what would settle it. If we do not have the answer already, at least we know how to get it. Getting it might not be easy, if an inference from what we know now about Venus was not enough. Better fuels, metals or instruments would be needed for an exhaustive hunt and might cost more than we are willing to spend. But these matters of technique and willingness do not affect our understanding of what is involved. It is a matter of fact and one which we see how to decide.

The limiting case of a closed question is one where the answer is known already. The child asks what laid that speckled egg and is told, 'a thrush'. The pupil asks the date of the Magna Carta and is given the right answer; or asks something harder and is told to look it up in the library. These are questions which tap a stock of information and there is no mystery about them. They are like simple raids on the memory store of a computer. Call such questions *completely closed*.

Harder questions soon begin to tax the existing stock of information. What is $29,317 \times 82,401,379$? Perhaps no one has asked exactly that before and there is no file which holds the answer. But the technique is to hand and simple ignorance is soon dispelled. There are indefinitely many facts, which we could establish, if we wished, once armed with a suitable technique. Where we already have the technique, the questions which apply for them are almost completely closed too.

But matters of fact soon outstrip existing techniques. Are there little blue people on Alpha Centauri? That is quite beyond us at present. We can say that it is unlikely on the available evidence. But the space probe needed to decide is science fiction. On the other hand, it too is a straightforward matter of fact. It calls only for a ship powerful enough to travel so far to settle which of two clear possibilities in fact holds and, in principle, we know what would be involved in building such a ship. So that too can be deemed a closed question.

Notice those little words 'in principle'. They signal the start of a blurred edge to the idea of a matter of fact. Are there little blue people so far away in the universe that it would take a million years to get there? It is not clear whether we know how to find out. 'In principle' a long enough journey on a fast enough ship would do it. So 'in principle' would a ship with a space-warp-drive which jumped intermediate points. But these are not exactly real possibilities for us. On the other hand, mere distance seems not to make a difference. If it is a matter of fact whether there are fairies at the bottom of the garden, then it should be one whether there are fairies at the end of the next galaxy. 'In principle' it is the same sort of question. Let us say that it is closed without being completely closed. It is not completely closed because we neither have the answer already nor do we have the technique which would give us the answer. It is closed, none the less, because (to put it roughly for the moment) we can state conditions for the truth or falsity of the hypothesis about little blue people.

There is an image for closed questions, which may help to keep things simple. It is the image of map-making. The map-maker arrives at unknown country with a blank sheet of paper, explores and gradually records what the country is like. In olden times it might be as hard to explore the world as it is now to explore the stars. The map-maker might not know how to record the curvature of the earth; indeed might believe the earth to be flat. But, in principle, the landscape was out there waiting. Its mountains were so high, its rivers so long and it either did or did not contain dragons. The map-maker's problem was a well-defined one of reproducing things as they were. This is a powerful image for the nature of many questions in everyday life and in science. It applies not only to finding out how things are but also to deciding how they were or will be. Historians, for instance, cannot journey back in time but we usually think of them too partly as makers of maps, whose work stands or falls in principle by whether it is accurate. The image is of a world independent of what we believe about it, whose features are an ultimate and objective test of truth for what we believe. Wherever that image makes sense, questions are closed.

Open Questions

The image makes sense less often and less thoroughly than one might suppose. Is there conscious life elsewhere in the universe? Little blue people would be an example but, as noted, 'conscious life' embraces far more and there is soon a puzzle about what counts. Let the map of Alpha Centauri record 'Here be gaseous cuboids' and let us add all that observation can tell us of their behaviour. That may still leave us undecided whether they are a life-form and whether they are conscious. There seems to be something here which eludes map-making.

The obvious retort is that the question is at fault. It is like telling the map-maker to record all salient features without specifying what counts as salient or even what 'salient' means. Certainly that is a possible fault and one which can lead to wasted time. For instance, if a satellite were positioned permanently above Nebraska, there might be an argument about whether it circles the earth. It does, in that it orbits the earth's notional centre point; it does not, in that it has no path round the earth's surface. Which is the right answer? It really does not matter, as only the preferred use of the verb 'to circle' is at stake. But that is a deliberately trivial example and it will not generalize. More hangs on questions of what is to count as conscious life. If that is not plain for gaseous cuboids, try it for attitudes to the human foetus in arguments about abortion. Admittedly this is a moral matter and so may seem special but there is also a matter of how to conceptualize a foetus and that is a further question.

The new factor is that the country to be explored is no longer independent of our thought. Of course, the question whether there are mountains never was independent of what we mean by 'mountain' but this is not what I am after. Even if we refused to *call* Everest a mountain, it would still *be* one. Whether or not we call a 3,000-metre hill a mountain makes no difference to the landscape. But plenty of concepts do not function just as labels. Concepts also enter into how we perceive, before we interpret and explain. Indeed, in perceiving, we are often already interpreting and explaining. That is the link between what may have seemed very disconnected readings of the opening question. Travels in space, I said, might change our picture of space and our picture of ourselves. The link is that they might revolutionize our way of thinking about what there is, making us self-conscious first about our map, then about our ways of mapping and then about ourselves, who make the map. Instead of giving new decisions within a framework of thought, they could shift the framework. Closed questions are those, however difficult and important, whose answers only add to our information. Open questions threaten the rules by which we decide what to believe.

This distinction is more easily seen with the help of history. Let us give the question of life among the stars an older context. In medieval Christian astronomy the earth was the centre of the heavens, stationary and set within the concentric crystal spheres of the moon, the sun, the planets and the fixed stars. These spheres revolved eternally round the earth and only below the sphere of the moon was there any change or decay. This cosmology was not separate from the received view of life on earth. Both were entwined within a Christian framework, enmeshed with a view of human nature. Man was unique in the cosmos in being created with free will and a corruptible soul. He was at the centre of God's design both physically and spiritually. Physically, the earth was at the literal centre of things. Spiritually, he was the only reason why God had not created a fully automatic universe without place for choice between good and evil. Physical and spiritual were connected aspects of this central mystery. Within the framework there was something odd about asking whether there is conscious life elsewhere. Provided that the framework went unchallenged, the answer was plainly 'No'. To toy with the idea of other conscious beings, perhaps of other Gardens of Eden and even of other crucifixions, was plainly idle. To the closed question the answer was definite. Yet curiosity continued.

In fact, the framework was fragile and under growing pressure both religious and scientific. The strains which led to the Reformation subverted the traditional authority of the Catholic Church and, hence, its power to keep closed questions closed. Astronomers began to insist on a new map of the heavens, displacing the earth from the centre and, as it was put later, smashing the crystal spheres like windows. It became reasonable to ask whether there is conscious life elsewhere – a subversive, now open, question, which made serious sense but only as a fresh framework for it emerged. The process was gradual and argumentative. Indeed it was dangerous – heretics could find themselves burnt alive. The modern map of heaven and earth took the shape, which we now broadly accept, only in the sixteenth and seventeenth centuries. We can realize now, with hardly a tremor, that our earth is just a satellite in a tiny solar system barely 7,350 million miles across, embedded in a medium-sized galaxy of 100 billion stars, itself one in a web of galaxies to which our greatest telescopes can find no end. We can accept that human life has lasted a mere tick of the astronomical clock. To that extent we have a framework for the question.

With hindsight, we can see how a closed question can become open and then, within a new framework, start to become closed again. But it has not become wholly closed. We no longer insist on making human life central to an account which fuses science and religion. But we do not yet understand the nature of conscious life. Our own framework is vulnerable in its turn to future experience. At the same time, like any framework of thought, it governs experience. This is a puzzling relationship. The distinction between questions posed within a framework and those which challenge a framework is not going to come out tidily. We can make it with fair success by comparing different cultures in time (history) or place (anthropology). But a latent puzzle soon obtrudes, when we try to make it in our own case. We are enmeshed in our own ways of thinking; to raise open questions, we must be able to think that our ways of thinking may be wrong. There is something paradoxical about that sort of curiosity.

Paradox

I have been speaking of a framework of thought, as if it were always a complete and consistent ordering of general beliefs and rules for interpreting experience. If that was truly so, it would be hard to see how frameworks can change. In part, it is no doubt true that they yield to fire and sword, powder and shot. Also, they adapt to other changes in material life, in the economic forces of production

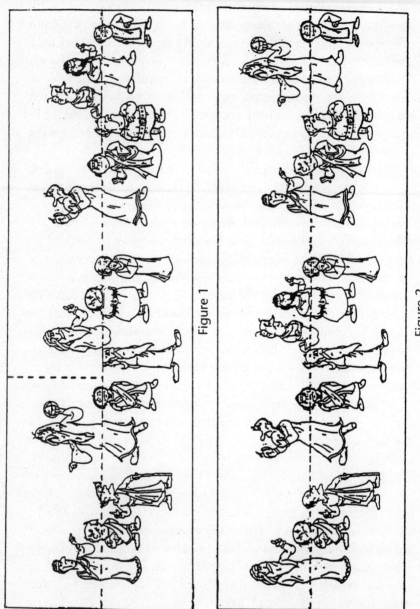

Figure 1

Figure 2

and in technology. But such pressures do not explain (or at least not fully) how people can come to think that their thought is wrong. An important element in the answer, I want to suggest, is paradox.

'Paradoxical' is often used to mean no more than 'odd' or 'surprising'. We call it paradoxical that elephants fear mice or that primitive languages can be more complex than advanced ones. This catches something of the idea by hinting at an underlying reason for surprise. But everyday paradoxes usually come complete with an explanation and that removes their power to subvert a framework. For instance, when the Victorians, moved by concern for better public hygiene, first purified the drinking water, they were disconcerted to find an increase in pulmonary tuberculosis, the killer disease better known as consumption. It was paradoxical to find that better hygiene kills. Nor was the correlation a coincidence. The explanation, however, was that, with the water purified, people were drinking less milk; half the cows at the time had bovine tuberculosis; this bovine variety is nasty but not fatal for humans and it immunizes against the pulmonary kind; so the defence supplied by the milk had been weakened. The paradox thus vanished, yielding new knowledge and without subverting the principles of hygiene. But not all paradoxes have such local effects.

A paradox, to put it formally, is a pair of statements, each with strong reasons but which cannot both be true. Let us pick out the formal point with a light-hearted example and then look at a paradox which is both famous and stubborn.

Figure 1 is a picture of 15 philosophers, each busy pondering some deep riddle of existence. If it is cut along the dotted lines and the pieces are shuffled round, we get figure 2. No sleight of hand is involved: both pictures have all and only the same parts, as a spot of work with photocopy and scissors will prove. Yet the 15 philosophers have mysteriously become 14. So there is strong reason to think that one has vanished and also strong reason to think that none has vanished. For, given that

(1) There were 15 philosophers
and (2) There are 14 philosophers
conclude (3) *One has vanished*

and given that

(1) There were 15 philosophers
and (2′) Nothing has been added or subtracted
conclude (3′) *None has vanished.*

There is no disputing (1), (2) or (2′); yet (3) and (3′) cannot both be true. Or so it seems. It would spoil the fun to say more (although the reader might care to decide which one has vanished) and, meanwhile, that picks out the logic of a paradox neatly enough.

Now let us look at the stubborn example. The idea of human freedom is a source of old and fertile paradoxes. One arises from the idea of an all-knowing, all-powerful God who has created everything in the universe, including man, and has given man free will. Given that

(1) God is the all-knowing and all-powerful Creator
and (2) God has given us free will
conclude (3) *We are sometimes responsible for what we do.*

On the other hand, given

(1) God is the all-knowing and all-powerful Creator
and (2′) Every event has a cause
and (3′) What is caused could not have been different
and (4′) Anyone who acts freely could have done otherwise
conclude (5′) *We are never responsible for what we do.*

This is not nearly as neat an example as that of the vanishing philosopher. It involves more assumptions (stated and hidden), its logic is not as tight and the exact source of trouble is up for dispute. Some thinkers have denied that there is a paradox, since one half is merely fallacious. Others have argued ingeniously that the two conclusions can be combined, given a right reading of the supports. These matters are the topic of chapter 9. But the paradox has been very stubborn – the core of it does not depend on a belief that there is a God – and, for the moment, I shall take it as a genuine case of two conflicting statements each supported by strong reasons.

This happens when a framework of thought combines two distinct ways of picturing a single world. The world contains a history of human actions which we regard, from the standpoint of ethics and everyday psychology, as performed by free agents who could have chosen otherwise. Our whole view of what has meaning and value in human life seems to depend on it. On the other hand, human actions are events in the world of cause and effect and, even if they are effects of will, we do not suppose that the will works at random. So, from the standpoint of science, we are inclined to think of our actions as determined by their inputs plus the causal laws of nature. Our whole view of human life as something ordered and explicable seems to depend on it. Each standpoint separately makes a good deal of sense and, certainly, has far stronger reason to keep to it than to abandon it. Yet each seems to exclude the other. The conflict need not be obvious from the first but, once it obtrudes, it is intolerable.

There follow attempts to undermine the paradox but, let us continue to suppose, they fail. Something in the framework then has to give. But what? It now becomes important that the paradox is not precise. I stated it as one arising for a conception of God, which permeated all departments of life. Historically that is how it has come down to us. So it would be reasonable to expect that a firm distinction between science and religion, of the kind now common-place, would remove much of the pressure. Historically, however, it has not really done so – the previous paragraph discussing science and ethics did not mention God once and, besides, puzzlement about free will is older than Christianity. So it can happen that a framework changes in response to a paradox and yet manages to take the paradox with it.

Hindsight thus has its pros and cons. It helps in seeing the difference between closed and open questions by showing that frameworks exist and change. Sometimes we can watch a paradox arise, strain its framework to breaking point and then be resolved by a new framework. For example the Victorian concern for hygiene relied on a modern conception of disease as the work of micro-organisms and particles, within a picture of nature as a mechanical system of cause and effect. We can contrast this way of thinking with an earlier one in which disease was reasonably held to be a divine punishment for sin and hence a suitable matter for prayer. We can also present the later framework as a solution to intolerable intellectual puzzles set by the earlier. But hindsight also has its snags. It tempts us to think of intellectual changes as always an advance and it makes us forget that we too have a framework. That we do is crucial for this book and the fact that we cannot step aside from our own framework is the crucial point about philosophical thinking.

Earlier, I could not give a crisp test for whether a question was closed or open. That was because I cannot give a crisp definition of a framework. Loosely, we can see that theorizing about anything goes on within a set of assumptions, some broader than others. For instance, space rockets are designed on a theory about metals and fuels, which, in a sense, is the framework of the enterprise. But that theory rests in turn on a wider physics, which relies on much more general assumptions about matter and energy. Even the assumptions of physics, however, presuppose a very broad account of truth, logic and the nature of knowledge and hence of human understanding. If these widening frames of reference were simply nested like Chinese boxes, then a 'framework of thought' would simply be the largest box. Alas, things will not turn out to be as straightforward as this. So, for the moment, let us just say that a paradox subverts a set of very general assumptions by showing that they cannot all hold at once.

Vision

So something has to give. Creative wonder is a search for order and meaning. We want our experience to make sense. On the surface it is often fragmented or pointless. To the untutored eye the night sky is in arbitrary motion. Life lasts only a cosmic instant, before being lost in an uncaring void. Yet experiences without sense are intolerable. The turning of the seasons, the fall of the sparrow, the death of a friend need to be found significance. Frameworks are more than an attempt at tidy principles of organized thought. They are also an attempt to find sense under the surface of what we perceive and feel. They express a vision.

Here too it is easier to see from a distance. As an example, let us take an eighteenth-century vision preserved for us in Alexander Pope's *Essay on Man* (1734). It is an optimistic vision of nature as a realm which makes complete and satisfying sense to a devout mind. Pope captures it especially well in these four lines:

> All nature is but art unknown to thee;
> All chance, direction which thou canst not see;
> All discord, harmony not understood;
> All partial evil, universal good.

His hope is that a surface, which may seem to us marked by chance, discord and evil, is in truth an expression of art, direction, harmony and good. There is design in everything, if we but look hard enough. God has created the world as an artist creates. He has ordered everything so that even what looks random is really the due effect of its cause. If we think that there is wanton ugliness and coarse, cruel destruction, then we do not grasp the whole, rather as the novice cannot hear the harmony in strange music. Partial evil always makes sense when seen in God's larger plan for the greatest good. The next two lines conclude triumphantly:

> And, spite of pride, in erring reason's spite,
> One truth is clear, whatever is, is right.

Most of us do not now share this vision, except perhaps in a casual, speech-day sort of way. In particular, we do not equate order as laws of cause and effect with order as divine purpose or order as moral significance. We no longer hope or expect to theorize ourselves into a kind of moral attunement with the universe at large. Instead, we theorize dispassionately about a universe which, we may well believe, has no moral order built into it at all. We tend to separate the order of things from the meaning of human life. But theorize we still do. We still connect specific areas of our thinking in an effort to build larger but coherent pictures and we still try for a single picture free of paradox. The pursuit of truth takes many forms and each can be questioned or refused. But we must pursue it somehow: without some vision we die.

That all leaves a powerful tension between experience and vision. Experience does not dictate vision – we can always find in experience the sort of order which we are determined to find. On the other hand, vision is vulnerable to experience as well as to paradox. That is a fact both about science and about our moral passage through life. So, once again, it is not possible to be crisp and clear even in the opening chapter. But I hope that a reasonably definite theme has emerged. At any rate, I shall summarize it and then say what is coming in the other chapters.

Summary

Is there conscious life elsewhere in the universe? On the face of it this is a closed question, one which turns on a technical matter of scientific fact and sets problems of method only because the universe is large. That is a useful start, since the idea of questioning for purposes of map-making is a clear and familiar one. But it takes us only so far. A closed question asks for information within an existing framework and, at some indefinite point, such requests challenge the framework itself. At that point an open question is posed, one which also wonders how it is to be answered.

Open questions can arise just because knowledge is very incomplete. Ancient man asks why the sun rises and finds that no one has the makings of an answer. But, more likely and more interestingly, he is given an answer about the chariot of the sun and the ways of the sun god and the answer does not satisfy him. He sets it against the answers to other questions and notes that they cannot all be true. So he asks for a standpoint from which to umpire and finds that there is none. He has hit on a paradox, which will persist at least until the framework changes.

A framework is a set of assumptions and rules of order. It governs what we make of experience and supplies our broadest picture of the reality, whose surface experience presents. That is Vision and the reasoned effort to achieve it is the daunting aspect of philosophy. But this is not the note on which I want to end the chapter. An outline of what is in later chapters will, I hope, give a promise of enjoyment too.

The next chapter is about the arts of argument, an invitation to Logic. It discusses inference, evidence and analogy, describes some fallacies and adds to what has already been said about paradox. Then there are three chapters about the mind's understanding of nature or the problems of Knowledge (or Epistemology). Here, the tension between framework and experience is taken up in more detailed and vivid ways, starting with Plato's allegory of the Cave and ending with a recent image of knowledge as a web of belief. That leaves an obtrusive puzzle about the self, as a link to chapters 6–8. It seems that all knowledge rests on consciousness and involves a self, which knows. This obtrusive self interferes with our hope of objective truth in science but is crucial for an understanding of human life and of ethics. Chapter 6 conducts a hunt for the self, which slips away in the attempt to relate the inner world to the outer, and the next two chapters try to pin it down in our moral understanding and ideas of freedom in social life. By that time both sides of the freewill paradox will be ready for action and the final chapter will wrestle with them, although not to a tidy finish.

Invitations beckon and Introductions point. An introduction should provide a sketch of a landscape and a map of the start of the main paths into it. It should be judicious and informative. Introductions to Philosophy are the devil to write, because all aspects of topic and method are in dispute. Happily I have not had to try, although

I would be sorry if a professional philosopher chanced on the book and thought it too irresponsible. Thus the periodic remarks about Vision are a gesture to Metaphysics. The chapters on knowledge lay out traditional disputes between rationalism and empiricism, followed by new ones which result from denying the need for knowledge to have foundations. The discussion of mind, body and persons is a foray into the Philosophy of Mind. Moral Philosophy is broached in chapter 7, and the way opened to Political and Social Philosophy in the next. That leaves some blanks – the Theory of Meaning and Aesthetics, for instance – but I hope that enough academic philosophy is in evidence to tell a prospective student what to expect.

None the less an Invitation can afford to be more personal and readier to lay itself open to dispute. So the reader should refuse to be put upon. There are scores of other absorbing topics and worthy approaches, if you do not care for mine. There is no reason why you have to agree with what I say, just because it is here in solemn print. The book is for do-it-yourself enthusiasts and its work will be done, if the subject at the end has the fire and fascination which I find in it myself. At that point I hand over to others.

2

Reasoning

It may not have struck you that at least two Maoris have the same number of Maori friends. But it is certainly true and I shall prove it in a moment. First, we need some general remarks on the principles of reasoning and a few logical tools.

This is a chapter about argument, in the sense of the giving of reasons for a conclusion. A judge who invites further argument on a point is asking the lawyers in court for persuasive reasons to accept or reject it. Some kinds of persuasion are not being invited. The lawyers are not expected to produce a shotgun or used banknotes in a plain envelope as inducements to decide in their favour. Nor does the judge wish to be gulled by rhetoric, lies or fallacies. Each side is being invited to demonstrate that, given what is already common ground, a fair-minded judge cannot reasonably refuse to come down on their side. The demonstration must show that there is a path from *premises* to *conclusion*, which abides by the rules of sound reasoning.

These rules are not altogether clear-cut; nor, when they are, is it always clear what counts as applying them. Reasoned judgement does not always have the decisive clarity of a computer program and especially not in philosophy. But there are some important ground rules. I shall lay them out under the titles of 'Proof' and 'Evidence' and then combine them in order to discuss the kind of reasoning which marks scientific work. The root difference between proof and evidence (as I shall use the terms) can be seen in these two arguments:

(A) 1st premise: Most Maoris are brave
     2nd premise: Most Maoris are loyal
     ───────────────────────────────────────
     Conclusion: At least one Maori is brave and loyal.

(B) 1st premise: Some Maoris are brave
     2nd premise: Some Maoris are loyal
     ───────────────────────────────────────
     Conclusion: At least one Maori is brave and loyal.

In (A) logic guarantees the conclusion, given the premises, and that is a matter of *Proof*. In (B) logic gives no guarantee but the premises offer some *evidence* for the conclusion. Since it is, as it happens, very poor evidence, you might suppose that (B) is an example from the bottom of a scale with (A) at the top end and examples with goodish evidence ranged in between. But the difference is not simply a matter of degree. The next two sections of the chapter will make this clear and the third will be about scientific method.

Proof

The logical soundness of an argument depends solely on how premises relate to conclusion. One could not object to the *logic* of argument (A) by claiming that most Maoris are cowards nor even by showing its conclusion to be false. The logic of (A) claims only that *if* most Maoris are brave and most are loyal *then* at least one is brave and loyal.

Suppose you had to demonstrate the logic of (A) to someone who did not see it. You might start by picking a number, say 11, and demonstrate it for that. If at least 6 are brave and at least 6 are loyal, then at most 5 are brave but not loyal; so at least one brave Maori is also on the list of loyal ones. This would not take you very far. Perhaps 11 is a special case. So you might let the other person pick any number, since, however many are tried, none will be found where the premises could be true and the conclusion false. But this too is not enough. Perhaps there is a fatal number as yet unpicked. A general guarantee is needed to show that there *cannot* be exceptions.

So you must prove the soundness of the argument for all possible cases. The premises say that at least half-plus-one of all Maoris are brave and at least half-plus-one loyal; so at least one brave Maori is on the loyal list. That shows it *impossible* for the premises to be true and the conclusion false. The conclusion *follows logically* from the premises.

(B) has 'some' in the premises, in place of 'most'. That changes the soundness of the argument. Exceptions are now possible. For instance, if there were a total of 11 Maoris, 5 could be brave and 5 loyal (thus making the premises true) and none would need to be brave and loyal (thus making the conclusion false). In general, the premises of (B) say that at least one is brave and at least one is loyal; and that carries no logical implication that at least one is both. So (B) is logically unsound.

That does not end the matter, however, as can be seen from

(C)   1st premise: Many Maoris are brave
      2nd premise: Many Maoris are loyal
      Conclusion: At least one Maori is brave and loyal.

Is (C) sound or unsound? That seems an easy enough question. 'Many' is a vague term. In some uses it implies 'most', making (C) a version of (A) and sound. In other uses it implies 'more than a few', making (C) a special case of (B) and so unsound. Hence (C) is indeterminate, but sound in some versions and unsound in others.

You might retort that this misses the point. To decide the merits of (A) there was no need to visit New Zealand or think about Maoris at all. The same goes for deciding that (B) does not pass the test which (A) passes. But (C) does demand some information about Maoris. Given that they are not unlike other groups of people, it is reasonable enough to draw that conclusion from those premises. (B) can be read as a weak version of (C) rather than merely as a flawed attempt at (A).

That is perfectly true and it shows that logic is not the only test of an argument. In (C) the premises do not imply the conclusion but they make it (fairly) likely. (C) is a matter not of *proof* but of *good evidence*. Where proof is at issue, an argument is either sound or unsound absolutely. Evidence, on the other hand, allows degrees of soundness, with conclusions being more or less likely on the evidence of the premises and its being more or less reasonable to accept the argument.

This use of 'proof' to refer strictly to the logic of arguments is taken from mathematics and there is a risk of confusion. A mathematician cannot *prove* a conclusion merely by showing it very likely. In courts of law and everyday life, however, 'proof' is used less formally. For instance, if George is accused of stabbing Henry in London at 3 p.m. and can show that he was in Glasgow at 2.45 p.m., he has proved his innocence. No jury which accepts the premises of this 'proof' could reasonably convict him. Yet nothing in logic alone stops a person from travelling 400 miles in 15 minutes. So, for the purposes of this book, George has overwhelming *evidence* that he is innocent but not *proof*. There is, of course, nothing sacred about the use of words but the underlying difference matters.

Here are two more proofs:

(D) (1) If Martha were a witch, she would not have drowned
    (2) She drowned
∴ (3) She was not a witch.

(E) (1) If all our actions are predictable, we do not have free will
    (2) We have free will
∴ (3) Not all our actions are predictable.

It is important that (D) and (E) stand or fall together. They are examples of the same argument. There was no need to visit New Zealand to see whether, given that most Maoris were brave and most loyal, there is at least one brave and loyal Maori. That was because the argument really had nothing to do with Maoris. It depended only on the logic of 'most'. Equally (D) is not really to do with witches nor (E) with free will. Both depend only on the logic of 'if . . . then' and 'not'. Both strip down to a working skeleton:

(F) (1) If p then q
    (2) Not-q
∴ (3) Not-p

where p and q are dummies for whatever statements you please.

Logic studies such skeletons and its guarantees attach to the skeletons, rather than to the flesh put on them in examples. Similarly, the mathematician who draws a triangle with sides of 3 cm, 4 cm, 5 cm and *proves* it right-angled (as opposed to measuring its largest angle with a protractor and noting that it is right-angled) is relying on a general theorem for all triangles whose sides are in 3:4:5 proportions. Of necessity, all triangles with sides a, b, c, where $a^2 + b^2 = c^2$, are right-angled, as implied by Pythagoras' theorem. Proof is always general, abstract and involves necessity (whereas evidence is particular, concrete and a matter of likelihood).

Why, then, is (F) a sound argument? In the end that is a very deep question, since the source of the necessity in logic is neither obvious nor agreed. Without tracing the source, I would not want too much read into my remark that it is the skeleton which does the work. But, in the meantime, we can say something useful about (F) by introducing the idea of a *contradiction*.

In nice, simple thrillers the detective asks the suspect, 'Don't you know that your wife was killed last night?' and the suspect replies, 'News to me! How terrible! Who shot her?' He has been caught knowing what he claims not to know. He has (implicitly) contradicted himself. So would anyone who asserted the premises of a logically sound argument and denied its conclusion. This thought offers one neat and powerful way of proving an argument logically sound, namely to suppose the conclusion false and then deduce a contradiction.

For instance try supposing that the drowned woman in (D) was a witch. That gives us

>   (1) If Martha were a witch, she would not have drowned
>   (2) She drowned
> Suppose (3′) She was a witch.

Here if (1) and (3′) are true, she did not drown and (2) says she did.
So (1), (2), (3′) sum to a contradiction and cannot all be true. So, if
(1) and (2) are true, (3′) is false. That proves the original (3) *She was
not a witch* follows from (1) and (2).

> Similarly for (F):
>   (1) If *p* then *q*
>   (2) Not-*q*
> Suppose (3′) *p*

yield both *q* and not-*q* and hence cannot all be true. So not-*p* follows
from (1) If *p* then *q* and (2) Not-*q*.

This may seem a tiresome way of complicating an obvious point.
So here are two rather more effective examples of the technique and
then a very powerful one. First, the Maoris of the original argument
(A) come out now like this:

>   (1) Most Maoris are brave
>   (2) Most Maoris are loyal
> Suppose (3′) No Maori is brave and loyal
>   ∴   (4′) Less than half are loyal (from (1) and (3′)).

Since (4′) contradicts (2), that proves the soundness of

> (A) (1) Most Maoris are brave
>   (2) Most Maoris are loyal
> ─────────────────────────────────
>   ∴ (3) At least one Maori is brave and loyal.

Second, I began by promising to prove that at least two Maoris
have the same number of Maori friends. Very well, suppose
otherwise. Suppose that no two Maoris have the same number of
Maori friends. In that case, of *n* Maoris, one has *n*−1 as friends, one

has $n-2$, one has $n-3$ and so on, until we reach the last who will have to have no friends among the rest. But this is contradictory, since, if one has no friends, another cannot be friends with all (i.e. have $n-1$ as friends).

You might want to pick a hole on the grounds that one can be one's own friend or that a can be a friend of b without b having to be a friend of a. It is not wholly clear to me whether normal English would support you. This illustrates the point about skeletons. The work of the argument is in fact done by the properties of what logicians call irreflexive, symmetrical relations. An irreflexive relation is one which nothing can have to itself (like 'being bigger than' or 'being the father of'). A symmetrical relation is one which a has to b if and only if b has it to a (like 'being the same size as' or 'being a cousin of'). Logic guarantees that n things cannot each have an irreflexive, symmetrical relation to a different number of the others. There is, however, an element of judgement in deciding whether friendship fits the bill and I shall return to this element later.

Third, let us see why there cannot be a highest prime number. This is a much harder example to follow but also a far more striking one. A prime number is one which can be divided without remainder only by itself or by 1. Other numbers have primes as factors. For instance, 5, 7, 11, 13, 17, 19, 23 are primes, whereas 6, 8, 9, 10, 12, 14, 15, 16, 18, 20, 21, 22 have (various) prime factors. With very large numbers it becomes hard to decide whether they are primes, since there are more and more smaller numbers by which they might or might not be divisible. So it is plausible to suggest that all numbers above a certain size have factors. Here is the nub of a beautiful proof by Euclid, the Ancient Greek mathematician, that it is not so.

Suppose that there is a highest prime. Suppose, in other words, that P_1, P_2, P_3, P_4 . . . up to P_n are all the primes, with n as a finite number. (In yet other words, the series 1, 2, 3, 5, 7, 11, 13, etc. comes to an end.) Now multiply all the primes together, add 1 and call this number S. Then ask whether S is prime. If it is, then, since S is larger than P_n, it follows that the series does not end with P_n. If S is not prime, it has prime factors. But its factors cannot be on the list of primes up to P_n. This is because if x is divisible by y and y is greater than 1 then $(x + 1)$ is not divisible by y. So any factors of S are larger than P_n and once again P_n is not the highest prime. Hence it is contradictory to suppose that there is a highest prime number.

This technique of proof is known as *reductio ad absurdum* (making an assumption and deducing impossible consequences). I could give many other lovely examples. But that would only obscure the point, which is to bring out the sort of guarantee of a sound argument which logic requires and provides. The guarantee required is one to show it impossible for the premises to be true and the conclusion false. Where an argument has this kind of soundness, anyone, who grants the premises but denies the conclusion, lands in a contradiction. The art of logic is to strip arguments to their skeleton and demonstrate the contradiction. Formal logic is a set of techniques for performing this feat.

There is no need to be armed with all the techniques of formal proof before tackling the logic of actual arguments. Outside mathematics (including statistics) it is rare for arguments to turn solely on formal matters of any great complexity. But it is crucial to grasp what is involved in the idea of formal proof and to recognize some basic moves. Even the simplest inferences can set some instructive traps. For instance, from (1) If p then q and (2) p, it follows that q; and from (1) If p then q and (2) Not-q, it follows that Not-p. But p does not follow from (1) If p then q and (2) q; nor does Not-q follow from (1) If p then q and (2) Not-p. These last two cases are worth spelling out.

Sometimes arguments of the form (1) If p then q; and (2) q; so (3) p, can be tempting. For instance:

(1) If George is the murderer, he lied about his movements
(2) He lied about his movements
So (3) He is the murderer

might seem in order. So might a related argument using 'all':

(1) All numbers divisible by 6 are divisible by 3
(2) 42 is divisible by 3
_____
So (3) 42 is divisible by 6.

But it does not take long to realize that not only murderers lie about their movements and that many multiples of 3 are not divisible by 6. One way of pointing out the fallacy is to construct another argument of the same form with true premises and a false conclusion. For example:

(1) All numbers divisible by 6 are divisible by 3
(2) 39 is divisible by 3
_____
So (3) 39 is divisible by 6.

This is unsound and so, therefore, is the underlying form of it. Likewise (1) If p then q; and (2) Not-p; so (3) Not-q, will not do, as is made plain by:

(1) If a figure is a square, its inside angles add to 360°
(2)   is not a square
_____
So (3) Its inside angles do not add to 360°.

The same goes for (1) All dogs have four legs; (2) Cats are not dogs; so (3) Cats do not have four legs.

That gives us a useful way of refuting an argument. Find another of the same form which is obviously unsound and point out the similarity. This is not always decisive, since the similarity may sometimes be disputed. For example, when Alice says that 'I say what I mean' is the same thing as 'I mean what I say', the Mad Hatter retorts 'Not the same thing a bit! Why, you might as well say that "I see what I eat" is the same thing as "I eat what I see".' The March Hare adds 'You might as well say that "I like what I get" is the same thing as "I get what I like".' Both comments are disputable – it is not obvious that Alice 'might as well say' anything of the sort. Often there is an element of rhetoric and manoeuvre in trying to disprove arguments by drawing analogies with unsound ones. But that should not surprise anyone who tries to apply simple rules of logic to complex reasoning in everyday speech. Formal logic has its uses, as in a court of law, but only in a preliminary way. Beyond that, lawyers must *build* their case, *marshal* their evidence, *discredit* the other side. There are still tests of reasonableness but they are not mechanical.

Conversely, however, it can be very helpful to formalize everyday reasoning. Suppose someone says, 'Suicide must be wrong, because it is murder.' That is shorthand for:

	(1) Suicide is murder (of oneself)	All A is B
	(2) Murder is wrong	All B is C
So	(3) Suicide is wrong	∴ All A is C

The argument is sound. So, if you do not accept it, you must attack its premises. You might object that, since murder is the killing of *someone else*, suicide is not murder; or that, since murder is by definition *wrongful* killing, the second premise begs the question. In other words, logic is not the only thing which can go wrong with an argument and it is helpful to distinguish faults of logic from failures of other kinds.

Thus armed, let us tackle a famous and much disputed passage in ethics. It comes from John Stuart Mill's *Utilitarianism* (1861), in which he argues that an action is morally right in so far as it increases human happiness. (The principle involved is often called 'the greatest happiness of the greatest number'.) In chapter IV he sets about justifying this view of ethics and offers the following analogy:

> The only proof capable of being given that an object is visible, is that people actually see it. The only proof that a sound is audible, is that people hear it: and so of the other sources of our experience. In like manner, I apprehend, the sole evidence it is possible to produce that anything is desirable, is that people do actually desire it. If the end which the utilitarian doctrine proposes to itself were not, in theory and in practice, acknowledged to be an end, nothing could ever convince any person that it was so. No reason can be given why the

general happiness is desirable, except that each person, so far as he believes it to be attainable, desires his own happiness.

At first glance the passage offers a formal argument and an unsound one at that. Whatever is seen is visible, in the sense that it can be seen. By the same token whatever is desired *can be* desired. But that is not what matters, since the conclusion is supposed to be that happiness is desirable, meaning *worth* desiring. Mill seems to stand convicted of a fallacy.

On second thoughts, however, he does not exactly say that he has a proof. He claims to offer only 'the sole evidence it is possible to produce that anything is desirable'. In chapter I he has already remarked that 'Utilitarianism cannot have proof in the ordinary and popular meaning of the term' because 'questions of ultimate ends are not amenable to direct proof'. He adds, however, that 'considerations may be presented capable of determining the intellect either to give or withhold its assent to the doctrine: and this is equivalent to proof'. The matter of substance here is whether the moral worth of an action can truly be settled by how well it promotes the greatest happiness. It will come up in chapter 7. Meanwhile let us focus on the point about 'sole evidence' and its being 'equivalent to proof'.

Mill is certainly right to grant that the analogy between visible and desirable does not yield a direct proof. People can desire what is undesirable but they cannot see what is invisible. But it is at least plausible to cite the fact that you want something as a reason why you should have it. You can plausibly argue for instance that on the whole what you want is good for you or that, other things being equal, you are entitled to make your own choice. Such moves support your conclusion, without proving that it follows. That is as far as we can go at the moment, since we now need to dissect the notion of evidence. That will help but it will not tie up all the loose ends – a point which you might wish to check at the end of the chapter and then bear in mind for later.

Before leaving the section on Proof, I want to point out that even logic is prone to paradox. Here, firstly, is a teasing example, which

is a running source of articles in scholarly journals. It is known as
'The Surprise Test'.

A teacher tells her pupils 'You will be tested at 9.00 a.m. one day
next week up to and including Friday. I guarantee that you will have
no more than five minutes warning of the test.' She has it in mind,
of course, that if she walks in at 8.55 a.m. on, say, Wednesday, and
announces the test, her pupils will have had no reason to expect it.
But they reason as follows. 'She cannot leave the test until Friday, as
that would give us 24 hours warning after 9.00 a.m. on Thursday.
So, to keep her promise, she would have to set it not later than
Thursday. So, if it is not set by 9.00 a.m. on Wednesday, we again
have 24 hours warning. So Thursday is also out. So she cannot leave
it until Wednesday, for similar reasons nor, therefore, until Tuesday.
So she must set it on Monday and we shall be expecting it. So she
cannot set it at all.' Is this a proof? Well, it is a very tight chain of
reasoning and I challenge you to break it. On the other hand, the
upshot is absurd, as you will see, if you make it a matter of a year
instead of a week and ask whether she really cannot set the test in,
say, 113 days' time without breach of her guarantee. Which side
should we come down on? Logicians are still arguing and the puzzle
is starting to look like a genuine paradox.

An older example starts from the plausible idea that every
statement is either true or false (or at any rate not both). For instance,
if we write on a piece of card, 'Cats purr', that is a true statement and,
if we then write on the other side

'The statement on the other side of the card is true'

that is another true statement. But now suppose we rub out 'Cats
purr' and substitute

'The statement on the other side of the card is false'.

This has the odd result that each statement is true, if it is false, and
false, if it is true! Here too logicians are unsure which way to jump

(despite efforts to prove that no proper statement is on either side of the card).

These examples may look trivial but they (and others) undermine a natural belief that logic is a given and complete set of consistent rules of reasoning which we discover. On the other hand, there is also trouble if we think of logic as rules which we construct or invent. For instance, it should be possible to divide any set of things you please into two groups one with and the other without any property you please. For example, words should be divisible into one group – call it 'autologous' – which describe themselves, like 'short', 'polysyllabic', 'English' and another – call it 'heterologous' – which do not describe themselves like 'long' (which is not a long word), 'monosyllabic' (which is not a monosyllabic word) and 'French' (which is not a French word). But now try it with 'heterologous'!

Logic and mathematics have a history. They change in part because people hit on new and more powerful techniques – witness differential calculus in the seventeenth century or the evolving computer languages of our own. They change also, however, because they run into paradox from time to time and I hope that even these small examples show how disconcerting that can be. But, despite paradoxes, and despite the need to use human judgement when applying logic, there are some unchanging ground rules. They depend on the basic ideas which we have been considering – those of logical soundness, contradiction and *reductio ad absurdum*. They are summarized on p.53.

Evidence

Proof is a matter of showing what follows from premises, whether or not the premises are true. Knowledge of how the world works does not come into it, since a proof holds (or does not hold) in complete abstraction. *If* most Maoris are brave and most are loyal, *then* at least one is both; and that is because, if most of a population is in class X and most in class Y, then classes X and Y must intersect.

The marshalling of evidence is not so remote a business. Let us start with a daring example of the art.

The scene is the Diogenes Club in London's Pall Mall, where Sherlock Holmes is meeting his formidable brother Mycroft. The encounter occurs in the story of 'The Greek Interpreter' (in *The Memoirs of Sherlock Holmes* by Sir Arthur Conan Doyle) and the narrator is the faithful, bemused Dr Watson.

> The two sat down together in the bow-window of the club.
> 'To anyone who wishes to study mankind this is the spot,' said Mycroft. 'Look at those magnificent types! Look at these two men who are coming towards us, for example.'
> 'The billiard-marker and the other?'
> 'Precisely. What do you make of the other?'
> The two men had stopped opposite the window. Some chalk marks over the waistcoat pocket were the only signs of billiards I could see in one of them. The other was a very small, dark fellow, with his hat pushed back and several packages under his arm.
> 'An old soldier, I perceive,' said Sherlock.
> 'And very recently discharged,' remarked the brother.
> 'Served in India, I see.'
> 'And a non-commissioned officer.'
> 'Royal Artillery, I fancy,' said Sherlock.
> 'And a widower.'
> 'But with a child.'
> 'Children, my dear boy, children.'
> 'Come', said I, laughing, 'this is a little too much.'
> 'Surely', answered Holmes, 'it is not hard to say that a man with that bearing, expression of authority, and sun-baked skin is a soldier, is more than a private, and is not long from India.'
> 'That he has not left the service long is shown by his still wearing his "ammunition boots", as they are called,' observed Mycroft.
> 'He has not the cavalry stride, yet he wore his hat on one side, as is shown by the lighter skin on that side of the brow. His weight is against his being a sapper. He is in the artillery.'
> 'Then, of course, his complete mourning shows that he has lost someone very dear. The fact that he is doing his own shopping looks

as though it were his wife. He has been buying things for children, you perceive. There is a rattle, which shows that one of them is very young. The wife probably died in child-bed. The fact that he has a picture book under his arm shows that there is another child to be thought of.'

The trick is worked by drawing analogies with the aid of experience. The date is about 1885 and a sun-baked veteran soldier would have served in India. A hat worn on the side points to cavalry, sappers or artillery. But cavalrymen walk differently and sappers are heavier. Married men do not generally do their own shopping. Children who like rattles do not want picture books. There are some elements of logical proof involved but the analogies depend on the world around. That is plain from the fact that they would not hold so well if tried nowadays.

Yet there is a clear process of reasoning (discounting a little for the sheer fun of the flying inferences). Sherlock Holmes himself describes it as 'observation and deduction'. (That is a confusing label, if one knows that logicians use 'deduction' to refer to logical proof, as in the last section, and 'induction' for the kind of inference we are now going to talk about. But it captures the popular view of detection nicely.) Reasoning on evidence does not have the seal of logic. If the man outside the window were the villainous Moriarty in disguise, Sherlock and Mycroft could be right in all their premises and wrong in all their conclusions. That would make it plain that their inferences were all logically unsound; but it would not show a misuse of evidence, unless they should have spotted him for Moriarty. This is the difference between a *possible* mistake, which upsets a proof, and a *probable* mistake, which points to defects in evidence.

It is easiest to grasp the difference, if we try to lay the reasoning out logically and then see what is missing. Take Mycroft's remark, 'That he has not left the service long is shown by his still wearing his "ammunition boots", as they are called.' How exactly does this support the claim that the man is an old soldier,

very recently discharged? Well, we might suppose that Mycroft is
reasoning:

    (1) Only soldiers, present or past, wear ammunition boots
    (2) Past soldiers in ammunition boots have not been long
         discharged
    (3) This man is wearing ammunition boots and is not a serving
         soldier
  So (4) He is not long discharged.

That is a logically sound argument, arriving at the conclusion
desired. But, on reflection, the premises will not do. They are wider
than the conclusion and harder to establish – Mycroft neither
knows nor needs to know that they are strictly true. Also, the
premises are true, only if the conclusion is true, and he cannot
assume that the man is not an exception in order to prove that he
conforms to the pattern! So try something less question-begging, of
the form:

    (1) All (or most) *other* members of class X are also members of
         class Y
    (2) This man is a member of class X
  So (3) He is a member of class Y.

This catches better the idea of generalizing from experience or
drawing analogies. It is logically unsound, however, since there is no
contradiction in supposing that the man is unlike other Xs. So in
what sense is it none the less sound?

    The answer, you may well say, is that there is a cause or reason why
these Xs are Ys. Mycroft is relying not on the *mere* fact that
ammunition boots are worn by soldiers but on the *explanatory* fact
that ammunition boots are part of soldiers' uniform. I am sure that
this is crucial. For instance, Victorian logic textbooks used to instruct
readers to infer that all swans are white from the fact that all known
swans are white. This was an example of sound argument from
evidence, until black swans were discovered in Australia! It was then

clear that there had been presumed to be a *cause* or *reason* why swans are white, a presumption exposed and shot down by the sighting of black swans.

In that case, however, there is not much to say about the use of evidence which is both general and precise. With logical proof we saw that there are general skeletons of a precise kind. In logic, any argument of the form, for instance, *All X are Y and all Y are Z; so all X are Z*, is logically sound. But there is no similar general licence to infer that *whenever known Xs are Ys then the next X will be a Y*. We may infer it when there is cause or reason for *X* to be *Y*s and otherwise not. This is a sensible retort to anyone who hopes to give rules of evidence in parallel to the rules of logical proof. But in one important way it overstates the difference and thus threatens to make the study of scientific method impossible.

The difference is that logical inferences, being abstract, are not vulnerable to the facts of the world which we happen to live in: logic holds, as an old phrase has it, in all possible worlds. Evidence, on the other hand, is good evidence only if there happen to be suitable connections in our experience. This is a fair point but, by making logical reasoning seem merely mechanical and contrasting it with the marshalling of evidence, it makes the latter sound unsystematic. What is mechanical about logic (or mathematics) is that a proof can be laid out so as to show it fully computable. But this does not mean that logicians or mathematicians work mechanically in their search for proofs. Conversely, the fact that there is an art to the marshalling of evidence and the identifying of causal connections does not exclude the use of computers and statistical techniques. Nor does the lack of formal proof for conclusions drawn from evidence mean that scientific method lacks all systematic rigour.

To bring this out, let us look next at the idea of probability. In part it is an idea belonging to the proof section of the chapter. For instance, how probable is it that, when a roulette wheel with the numbers 1–36 and one zero is spun, number 17 will come up? A logical answer is:

(1) There are 37 equiprobable outcomes
(2) 36 of them are not '17'
_____
So (3) The probability of '17' is 1:36.

Here there is a general formula for arriving at chances by comparing the number of favourable outcomes with the number of possible ones. (Thus the chances of getting an odd number are 18:19.) This sort of calculation is the subject of an elegant branch of mathematics.

Now suppose that you have been watching a game of roulette for some time and the number 17 has not come up at all. You may begin to wonder whether the chances for the next throw really are 1:36. You might think them either better (because 17 is overdue) or worse (because there seems to be a pattern). The first thought is either silly – the 'gambler's fallacy' – or too subtle for a preliminary discussion. Let us concentrate on the second. You wonder how probable it is that there really is a pattern. The natural suggestion is that the wheel is not true, so that there are not in fact 37 equiprobable outcomes. How likely is that, on the evidence of a long series?

Here we need to contrast the mathematical theory for computing the chances of actual series within the set of possible series with the pragmatic thought that the wheel is imperfect (perhaps fixed). There is no definite number of ways for a wheel to be untrue, just as there is no definite chance that it will rain on 4 July. It is only more likely (or less likely) on some evidence than on other. (I recall a San Francisco radio station which used to give the exact percentage chance of rain every day. When asked how they arrived at it, they replied, 'See here, there are ten guys in this office. If seven of them think it will rain, that makes a 70 per cent chance.') Similarly, there is no exact figure for the probability on Mycroft's evidence that the man was a newly discharged veteran. This does not mean, however, that Mycroft was being arbitrary or unsystematic.

Notice that we are concerned with probability *on the evidence*. If you ask for *the* probability that the man was a newly discharged veteran, then it is, I suppose, either 1 (if he was) or 0 (if he was not). Probability-on-the-evidence has two elements: one, often mathematically precise, for what follows if the evidence is good evidence; and one, not precise, for the evidence's being good. Thus the chance of 1:36 for a '17' at roulette is exact, only given that the wheel is perfect; and in practice there is no *exact* probability, since there is always some doubt about the fairness of any wheel. It might have seemed earlier that Mycroft's reasoning should have been from the premises about ammunition boots and so on to the conclusion: 'So *probably* he is a recently discharged veteran,' thus perhaps making the argument logically sound after all. I did not state it like this, because I wanted to keep the logical (or mathematical) and evidential sides of probability apart. Mycroft is claiming both that the evidence is good and that he has used it well. These are distinct claims.

Relatedly, an argument about probabilities can be refuted in two ways. Suppose someone shows you three cards, one red on both sides, one blue on both sides and the third red on one side and blue on the other. He shuffles and puts a random card face down on the table. Its back is red and he says, 'This is either the red/red card or the red/blue card. So there is an even probability that the hidden side is blue. But, as I like your face, I will sportingly bet my £5 against your £4 that it is red.' Would you do well to take the bet? The answer is 'No', for the reason that the chances are not even. The exact chance that the other side is red is in fact 2:1, as you will see, if you imagine the red/red card having its sides marked (A) and (B). You are looking either at the red/blue card or at side (A) of the red/red or at side (B) of the red/red. In two of these three equiprobable cases he wins. This is different from the famous 'Three Card Trick' where you are invited to bet which of three cards is the Queen of Spades and the snag is that, just when you have won a few times and are about to bet your shirt, the queen is going to be secretly replaced with another card. Here too the probabilities are being wrongly suggested but for a reason which you cannot put an exact figure to.

Here I cannot resist adding an infuriating example to show how teasing even simple-sounding questions of probability can be.

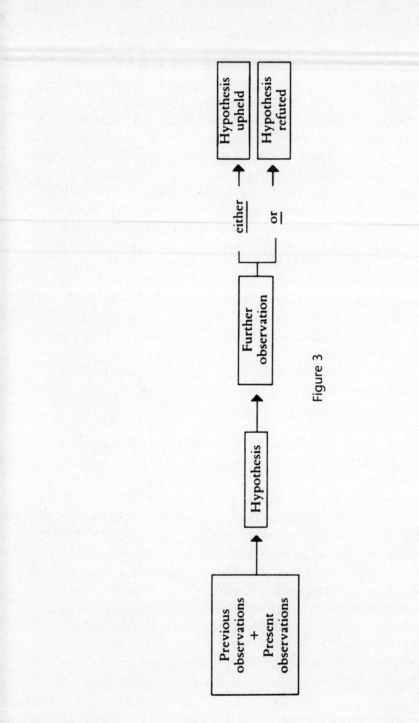

Figure 3

Suppose that you are the contestant in a television game show and find yourself looking at three doors. Behind one of them, you are told, is a Ferrari; behind each of the other two, a goat. You may open exactly one door and whatever is behind it is yours. So you pick a door at random and put your hand on the knob. But, before you can open it, the host intervenes. 'Wait,' he says, 'I know where the Ferrari is and would like to give you a bit more information.' He opens one of the other doors and shows you a goat. He then offers you the chance to change your door. Would you be wise or foolish to do so or does it make no difference? The question does not sound too hard but it has caused a national debate among probability theorists so heated that it reached the pages of *The New York Times*. Yet there is a definite answer and you might care to work it out. So as not to spoil the fun, I shall keep it to the end of the chapter.

Meanwhile, this part of the chapter is concerned with both the logical and the evidential sides of probability, but especially with the latter and what makes evidence good or bad. For this purpose, Mycroft is to be thought of not as offering a (somewhat hazy) calculation but as putting forward a hypothesis, which is likely to be upheld by experience. At its simplest, the detective process of 'observation and deduction' has the form of figure 3. The art in it consists partly in picking out a stable pattern in previous experience and partly in noticing the small present indications that this is a further example of the pattern.

It used to be said that there were definite rules for picking out patterns. For instance, the more soldiers Mycroft has seen wearing ammunition boots and the more civilians not wearing them, the better: the larger the number of Xs which are Ys, and the fewer the Xs which are not Ys, the likelier it is that all Xs are Ys and hence that the next X will be a Y: the greater the number of points of similarity between this new X and previous Xs, the likelier that this X also resembles the others in being a Y: and so on. This is not a silly attempt and it has led on to the technicalities of modern statistics, which are a major component of science. But it should not make us forget that the marshalling of evidence is an art. It is false that lumps of data can be fed into an automatic scheme and their significance extracted by cranking the rules. There is always an element of imagination and judgement needed. With this mildly subversive thought in mind, let us now turn to the logic of scientific reasoning. The rest of the chapter is a fairly innocuous preview of various matters which will turn thoroughly awkward, when taken up again in the three following chapters.

Scientific Method

Figure 3 connects present observation to past experience, thus allowing a hypothesis to be produced from which predictions can be made. That is certainly an important part of the use of evidence to support a conclusion and it catches the point that findings on evidence are subject to the verdict of experience, in a way in which logical proofs are not. But the diagram also suppresses much which is not simply a matter of noticing on the part of hawk-eyed detectives.

First, reconsider the plausible thought that the larger the number of Xs which have been Ys and the smaller the number which have not, the likelier it is that all Xs are Ys. This carries the misleading suggestion that evidence is a matter of large numbers of examples. Had Mycroft in fact previously noticed the boots of very many soldiers and the shoes of very many civilians? I doubt it and, anyway, it is not crucial. To revert to an earlier point, he was relying not on quantity but on a cause or reason. When Isaac Newton sat under a tree in the seventeenth century and was famously struck by a falling apple, he came up with the hypothesis that bodies attract each other in proportion to the inverse of the square of their distance apart. It would plainly be silly to picture him hastily recalling the behaviour of previous apples, or even (less silly but still misleading) of previous bodies of all sorts. He knew too few apples and too many bodies. There are infinitely many generalizations possible from a set of observations and the art of picking a likely pattern is not ruled by quantity.

What it is ruled by is more mysterious and I do not want to be led off into the psychology of great scientists (or detectives). But I am fairly sure that the art lies in spotting that, if something or other were so, then the event experienced would make sense. At any rate what the diagram certainly leaves out is the idea of a simplifying theory, which ascribes an elegant orderliness to what is experienced. The apple's falling and a million other very dissimilar events would all belong to the same simple pattern, if only there were what we now call the laws of gravity. The pattern is not written on the face of experience; imagination has contributed something which eyesight does not discern.

That somewhat poetic way of putting it does in fact gesture to Newton's psychology, since he believed deeply that God had ordained the hidden laws of mass and motion, which science tried to discover. But the point about imagination and the task of theorizing does not need the backing of religious belief. It needs only the thought that there is a conjecture involved in every use of evidence. The pattern is not read mechanically from the events but daringly imposed, with a highly selective warrant from past experience, not a routine one. That is why the impressive business of extracting patterns from data with the aid of powerful computer programmes is to be treated warily as a guide. It is true enough that computers can manage a complexity quite beyond us. It is less true that the human use of evidence is a pale effort at a vastly complex statistical pattern. The use of evidence is part of an attempt to make simpler sense of what is otherwise infinitely complex, and that requires imaginative conjecture.

We must, therefore, separate two further aspects of the use of evidence. One, known as 'the art of discovery', is the way in which scientists hit on their conjectures and hypotheses. The other, 'the logic of validation', is the way in which the merit of a hypothesis is assessed. Discovery is sometimes a very humdrum affair of look, see and crank the statistical handle, sometimes a wild leap in the dark,

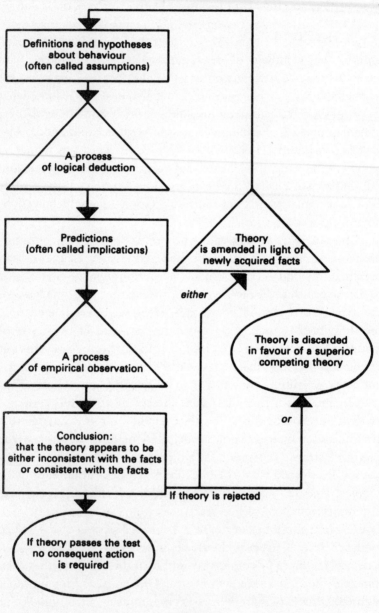

Figure 4

prompted perhaps by false belief, sometimes the result of a sheer accident, like a mix up in the chemical store. I shall not try to fathom the art here but Arthur Koestler's books, especially *The Act of Creation* (1964) and *The Sleepwalkers* (1959), are an exciting study of some dramatic episodes in the history of science, together with such general reflections as the study of an art permits. In so far as there are rules to follow for hitting on new ideas, there will also be a logic of discovery and many attempts have been made to lay some down. The best known is Karl Popper's *The Logic of Scientific Discovery* (1962); and his essay 'Conjectures and Refutations' (which is also the title of the book containing it) is an absorbing discussion of what logic can and cannot contribute. There is too much involved, however, for this chapter to tackle.

Once a conjecture is made or a hypothesis proposed, its merit needs to be assessed. That is easier to talk about. Figure 4 is a diagram, slightly adapted from P.E. Lipsey's *Introduction to Positive Economics* (1989), which lays out the skeleton of a common account. The basic idea is straightforward. For instance, starting with some knowledge of economic theory and of how consumers tend to behave, we infer that, if the price of gin rises relative to that of whisky, the demand for gin will fall. Then, given some figures, we predict the likely fall as exactly as we can. The prediction is put to the test of experience and is either upheld or refuted. If it is refuted, we either discard the hypothesis altogether or try an amended version. Thus, if the demand for gin in fact rises, something is drastically wrong but if it falls by the 'wrong' amount, we might be content with an adjustment.

The key points to notice are that the facts are the decisive test and that not everything involved in the prediction can be directly tested. The facts are decisive, because – it is very plausible to say – we do not know in advance how the world works and the whole purpose is to find out how, as a matter of fact, it does work. But, when we test, there are always several things at stake. To arrive at a prediction of the demand for gin, we had to assume that whisky is a substitute in consumers' eyes, that various laws of supply and demand hold, and so on. If the prediction fails, we have some choice about how to respond. The fault may be a narrow one confined to what we assumed about gin and whisky or it may go deeper into the larger economic theory which we were relying on. The choice of what to blame is not automatic – it verges again on an art – but, once made, it is to be tested against experience in its turn. There will be a further choice about how to read the results.

In this process, the most general propositions of economic theory are not directly tested. For instance, there is no direct way of testing whether it is true that, other things being equal, when price rises, demand falls. That will seem an absurd statement to make. What could be more obviously true than that people buy less when things cost more? Does it not happen all the time? Yes, it does. But there is a very important point about figure 4, which needs to be spelt out carefully.

Sherlock and Mycroft, looking out of the club window, are like speculative map-makers. They are producing a list of conjectures about the man outside, each of which can be tested separately and each of which may be true or may be false. 'Observation and deduction' is like making a map of an unknown land before exploring all of it. The landscape is as it is and the map is right or wrong accordingly. The map-maker who writes in 'Here be dragons' is taking a risk and waits upon the verdict of experience to settle whether dragons are there or not. Such risks are taken in the confidence that the unexplored will, on the whole, resemble what has been found in similar conditions. If the gum-trees in the known part of the forest contain koala bears, so probably do those in the unknown part. If travellers tell of dragons in explored parts of a distant continent, the early map-maker writes in dragons there and, no doubt, elsewhere too.

Economists and other scientists, however, are only in part like speculative map-makers. In other ways they are more like model-builders or producers of computer simulations. A model of an electron cannot try to mirror all or only the components, which experience will reveal, because we cannot observe electrons even in principle. A theory of animal instincts cannot be tested by observing instincts nor a model of the unconscious by peering into the unconscious. Sciences postulate unobservables, which have more in common with the gods of Homer than with the dragons on ancient maps. For (once the ancient Greeks knew that they would not find the gods by climbing Mount Olympus) the gods were posits, justified by showing how their posited existence made sense of experience, and not observable beings living in an unexplored corner of the world.

Models also have inner connections and lines of defence unlike maps. Suppose that we find two bodies which seem not to attract each other as stated in the laws of gravity. Would that show the laws to have been mis-stated? It certainly would not, at least not straight away. The first thought, no doubt, is that the measurements need checking. The next is that there is another body interfering – this was how the planet Neptune came to be discovered, after astronomers had been disconcerted to find neighbouring planets seeming to defy the Newtonian formula. The core of a major scientific theory can be defended for a long time against inconvenient facts by maintaining that things are not as they seem or by letting go of lesser hypotheses. Unexpected facts show that something is amiss – for example that instruments are inaccurate or that lesser assumptions are wrong or . . . or (only) finally that some major theory is at fault – but they do not point the finger at the major theory in particular.

That is why the most general propositions of economic (or any other) theory are not directly at risk. So, although it is plainly true that people buy less, when things cost more, this is not directly evidence for the proposition that, *other things being equal*, when prices rise, demand falls. Could other things be equal and yet demand sometimes increase when prices rise? When selling clothes to the rich, it sometimes pays to raise prices so as to make the garments seem more special and exclusive than the rival modes. When a staple food of the poor, like potatoes or rice, gets more expensive, often more of it is bought. (To buy the same amount the poor family must switch cash from other items, like meat, which it must then replace cheaply and so with more of the staple foods.) Such examples are cases of other things not being equal – or that is how economists choose to respond and thereby save the law of demand.

If a hypothesis does not risk failing a test, it is not exactly being tested. Ancient Greeks believed their affairs to be subject to the gods, who intervened as they saw fit. For instance, it was wise to sacrifice to Poseidon, god of the sea, before setting sail, as that would make him less likely to send a storm. There was no guarantee that Poseidon would oblige and, besides, there were other gods with power over weather, who might not see eye to eye with Poseidon. But a sacrifice helped. Now, suppose someone doubted that sacrifices made any difference, and was willing to doubt that the gods took any interest in human affairs or even that they existed at all. Could the question be put to the test? Well, in a loose sort of way, believers in the gods can always find evidence that they are at work. They can point to occasions when no proper sacrifice was made and a storm ensued, or when a calm voyage duly followed a proper sacrifice. Faced with counter-examples – sacrifice followed by storm, no sacrifice followed by a calm voyage – believers are not short of explanations. The sacrifice was badly performed, Poseidon was too displeased to be mollified, other gods had taken a hand. The exceptions prove the rule, since this way of reading them presupposes the truth of other beliefs about the gods. In short, experience amply confirms the proposition that, other things being equal, sacrifices help.

That does not end the matter, of course; the sceptic has been cheated of his point. The best way to complain is to say that no hypothesis is genuinely at risk. The defence that other things are not equal is so set up that it cannot be breached. The believer was not willing to state in advance what would refute the hypothesis and then to stick to it, if experience went against him. Experience, which could not have refuted a hypothesis, does not genuinely confirm it. The same goes for the deeper beliefs that the gods intervene in human affairs and, at the core, that the gods exist. These beliefs are not threatened by experience, which could not shake even the outlying belief that sacrifices help. Evidence counts in favour, only if other evidence would have counted against.

That is why I could say that there is no direct way of testing whether, other things being equal, demand falls, when prices rise. Yet the remark remains paradoxical. Demand plainly does fall, when prices rise (other things being equal). On the other hand, economic theory does rely on unobservables and does guard its predictions by adding 'other things being equal'. Besides, the believer in Greek gods can very easily say what would refute his hypothesis, for instance a clear demonstration that sailors who sacrifice are ship-wrecked much more often than those who do not. So how do we stop a sensible amendment to the 'observation and deduction' account of science from turning into an equally good picture of religious reasoning?

The question cuts very deep indeed. Most of us have been brought up on a story about how the progress of science has been at the expense of religion's claims to explain the world. For instance, where religion once held that cholera spread because people had sinned, we now know that plagues are spread because a micro-organism travels and multiplies. What is more, we can demonstrate it by medical cures. Religion is, in general, in retreat as a way of discerning *how* things happen and has become confined to explain-ing *why* their causes are set in motion. Religion has, on the whole, become a point of view, whereas science has become a handbook. But, when we think of the logic of science as one of models rather than of maps, we are forced to notice that religion has a logic too. What conclusions shall we draw?

There are, I think, three ways to jump. The first is hard-headed and pragmatic. It insists that scientific prediction works, whereas religious forecasts remain incurably vague. The second picks up an earlier point and leads into a discussion of the underlying reasons and causes of things. The third is to accept that science is, like religion, a point of view, with consequences which will be discussed mainly in chapter 5. I shall next say a little about each of these responses and then sum up the chapter in a limited and hard-headed way.

The first response is that, in so far as prediction in science works, we need not worry too much about the abstract differences between science and religion. For instance we can cure cholera with medicine but not with prayer and that is difference enough. This response is most effective in areas of science where there is little disagreement on matters of theory and it appeals most to those who are practically minded. It makes the purpose of using evidence less to arrive at truth and more to achieve control, less knowing and more doing. To echo the first chapter, it makes good sense for closed questions. This is because, with closed questions, it is usually not too hard to decide what to correct, when experience refutes a hypothesis.

But we have come too far to rest content with saying that science deals in closed questions and religion in open ones. Where a theory is in dispute, the lesson of experience is harder to read. For instance, doctors are divided about the roots of schizophrenia. Is it better viewed as a chemical imbalance in the brain or as a mental disturbance? The evidence is ambiguous, partly because it does not show how to control schizophrenia, partly because there is dispute about how to read it. It looks different, depending on the theoretical angle from which it is interpreted. Also, it is unclear what counts as control. For example is a drug-induced calm in the patient a mere suppression (perhaps dangerous) of symptoms or a way of treating the underlying condition? Doctors are more concerned to find the *truth* about the nature of schizophrenia than they might be, if it yielded easily to treatment. Similarly with cancer research, where success is limited so far, doctors are driven to probe deeper into the hidden working of cells and even into the mental or social condition of the sufferers. In this search for underlying causes, figure 4 is a far less definite guide to method and hence less of an obstacle to religious claims to knowledge.

That takes us into the second response, which sees evidence as a clue to causal forces and connections. Figure 4 suggests that the purpose of evidence is only to hit on a reliable pattern in events. Whereas Newton believed himself to have discovered a *force* of gravity, working according to *laws* of gravity, the diagram allows him only a general statement to the effect that bodies behave according to his formula. The difference is easy to word but subtle to analyse. It is a matter of whether the apple was caused to fall on Newton's head by an unobservable force or whether it merely instanced what always happens in similar conditions. One view makes the visible event the effect of an invisible force, the other makes the 'force' a shorthand label for a visible pattern. Each way of speaking connects with a broader philosophy and further discussion must wait until we have the broader picture. But, if science is a search for hidden causes, so is religion.

Before deciding whether the similarity is more than superficial, we should tidy a loose end. We noted earlier that there was no general reason to suppose that whenever known Xs are Ys then the next X will be a Y. It seemed sensible to comment that the inference held only if there was a cause or reason why known Xs are Ys. Even if all veterans known to Holmes had blue eyes, he would not be entitled to infer that the man outside had blue eyes, unless there was some strange biological law connecting blue eyes with military temperament or, more simply, an army rule that recruits must be blue-eyed. That is a sensible comment in the end, however, only if causes or reasons explain generalizations and are not merely the names of generalizations. We ordinarily think of causes or reasons as more than names of generalizations; but ordinary thought may be making a distinction which it cannot uphold. Figure 4 is, in effect, an attempt to do without it. It offers a way of finding out when we may infer from 'known Xs are Ys' to 'the next X will be Y' without positing hidden causes or reasons. Later on we shall be asking whether ordinary thought should be satisfied.

I have been careful to use the phrase 'cause or reason'. There may or may not be a crucial difference. That depends on whether the natural causes, which we try to find for the workings of nature, are importantly unlike the human reasons, which move human beings to action. The larger issue will be a later topic but there are some immediate points to make about our idea of evidence.

Evidence has a vital role in the sciences of nature and a vital role in such human business as the administration of justice or the writing of history. In courts of law there are rules of evidence and procedure which would be very odd as scientific rules. Witnesses must not report what other people have said to them, the defendant's 97 previous convictions must not be cited as evidence that he is likely to be guilty this time, and so on. In history the evidence that King Henry II did not in fact want Thomas Becket murdered (or that he did) can seem to depend less on whether other such *X*s are known to be *Y*s (are there any others?) than on what makes better unique sense of that particular period, viewed through the eyes of those historical actors. These are only preliminary points and it does not follow that, in the end, lawyers and historians do not follow the methods of natural science. But there is a surface difference to explore and some thinkers maintain that it goes very deep.

In that case the Holmes' method of 'observation and deduction' involves an understanding of social rules and an insight into motive. A closer look at the exchanges between Sherlock and Mycroft suggests as much. It is not simply that non-commissioned officers do have an expression of authority but that one goes with the job. There is a reason why a newly discharged veteran might wear ammunition boots. The way in which people in mourning dressed – normal practice then, although now largely dropped – was not a natural sign of grief, like tears or as a ring round the moon is a natural sign of rain, but a symbol of grief. Sherlock and Mycroft are reading the evidence as insiders, not as a visiting Martian would read it. They are identifying meaning and intention, whereas natural scientists do not ascribe meaning or intention to atoms. I do not propose to say much about the scientific study of social life in this book in a direct fashion. But I do in fact believe that it needs a notion of science more suited to history than to physics and have been careful not to pre-empt this view. Meanwhile it is worth keeping causes and reasons distinct.

It takes more than good eyesight to spot underlying causes or reasons. Nature requires a trained interpreter. Human affairs need an insider's view. The job of evidence is not just to link a present case to similar ones but to detect its origins. The same can be said of evidence in religion. Perhaps the hand of God can be known only by those receptive in spirit to its workings. Perhaps revelation is like a message between lovers, which those uninvolved cannot read. Even so, admittedly, there remain differences between scientific and religious interpretation and they may still turn out to run deep. Meanwhile, however, there are also similarities.

The third response is to accept the underlying kinship between science and religion. I shall not explore the implications now but instead give a fresh ground for making the response. As noted earlier, all evidence relies on some analogy between known cases and the present (or next) case. The principle involved has been called the Principle of the Uniformity of Nature and I gave a loose version of it when mooting it that 'if known Xs are Ys then the next X will be a Y'. It is hard, (perhaps impossible) to state the principle in a way that is both precise and plausible, but the idea is that the same pattern is always found in the same conditions. If we could not rely on it, everyday life would fall apart. We could not sanely boil an egg, buy a loaf, plant a seed, catch a bus, open a bank account or make a promise, unless we could count on tomorrow's world being broadly like today's and yesterday's. Every scientific experiment relies on it, every memory and attempt at history, indeed every naming of simple objects around us.

So, you might well suppose, one utterly basic task of a chapter on reasoning is to show why some such principle is sound. Disconcertingly, however, there seems no way to do it. We have been thinking about proof and evidence as the methods of justifying claims to knowledge. Neither will serve. To see why not, try constructing a sound argument with true premises and a Principle of the Uniformity of Nature as conclusion. For example:

(1) Science in the past has assumed that patterns repeat in the same conditions
(2) Science has been very successful

So ∴ (3) Patterns repeat in the same conditions.

This argument is not a proof, because nothing in logic stops the universe going haywire in a moment's time. If there were to be a sudden change in all patterns, the premises would be true and the conclusion false. That is the mark of a logically unsound argument. We could, of course, rule that out by building the conclusion into the premises but then we would be assuming what we were trying to prove. In any case, most philosophers would say, it is not the job of logic to guarantee that there is order in parts of the universe, far and near, large and small, past, present and future, which we have not witnessed. The job is one for evidence.

But evidence cannot do it either. It may seem that the past success of science is very good evidence that nature has the orderliness which science assumes. But it is any evidence at all only if we are already justified in inferring from past success to future success. Since this is precisely the kind of inference which we are trying to justify, we cannot rely on it, until we have justified it. That would be like arguing for the truth of the Bible by pointing out that the Bible claims to be divinely inspired. It would be another case of the fallacy of assuming what one is trying to prove in order to prove it. If all uses of evidence presuppose that things are, in general, orderly, then there can be no evidence for this presupposition itself.

The upshot is a paradox. On the one hand we could, it seems, hardly have better evidence that we live in an orderly universe and shall continue to do so. On the other hand we seem, on reflection, to have no evidence whatever, which supports this conclusion without assuming it. Many philosophers (and others) find this an incredible result and try to show that the challenge is a bogus one. But many have accepted that Reason cannot justify Reason and have tried to live intellectually with the result. David Hume, for instance, the eighteenth-century thinker, whose *A Treatise of Human Nature* (1739, Volume I, Part III) contains the most famous statement of the case, concludes that all our reasonings rest finally on custom and imagination. Similar thoughts have lately been causing upheaval in the philosophy of the sciences.

In the language of the first chapter, the basis of reasoning turns out to belong, it seems, to a framework or Vision, rather than to the store of human information. We started with closed questions about the uses of evidence but have ended with open ones. That is the sense in which science is, like religion, a point of view. But I do not want to leave the topic of reasoning without stressing that there is firm ground for the feet as well as clouds for the head. So let us finish with a down-to-earth summary.

Summary

Proof

1. An argument is logically sound, if its conclusion follows from its premises, in that it is contradictory to assert the premises and deny the conclusion.
2. A logically sound argument needs neither true premises nor a true conclusion; it requires only that, *if* its conclusion is false, *then* at least one premise has to be false.
3. One useful technique of proof is to suppose the conclusion false and deduce that the premises then cannot all be true. This is known as *reductio ad absurdum*.
4. Relatedly, a logically unsound argument can often be shown to be so by finding another example of its skeleton with true premises and a false conclusion.

Evidence

1. Sound uses of evidence rely on drawing analogies with known cases of the same pattern.
2. They are not a proof that the conclusion follows logically from the evidence: they show that the conclusion is probable on the evidence.
3. Probability statements are sometimes a matter only of logic and mathematics (e.g. there is a 1:13 probability of drawing an ace at random from a pack of cards). In this case they can be faulted only by errors in calculation.

4. Probability statements can also modify the strength of an analogy (e.g. the man outside was very probably a veteran). In this case they can be challenged by disputing the evidence, on the grounds either that it has been mis-stated or that it is poor evidence.

Scientific Method

1. The simplest picture compares science to map-making with the test whether the hypothesis describes the world correctly. But since this leaves no place for unobservables, a better comparison is with model-making or computer simulation.
2. The 'art of discovery' requires imagination and conjecture: the 'logic of validation' requires an objective test, which a hypothesis is not guaranteed to pass. A hypothesis which is guaranteed does not become more probable by being tested.
3. Not everything which a science assumes can be directly tested: refutations do not point the finger precisely. The 'logic of validation' is not wholly mechanical.
4. It is often presumed that patterns are significant in so far as they reflect a cause or reason for them. At this stage it is wise neither to accept the presumption nor to reject it. The same caution applies to the open question about the depth of the difference between natural causes and human reasons.
5. As a technique for answering closed questions, scientific method works by discarding or amending hypotheses when the predictions extracted from them fail.

PS   You double your chance of winning the Ferrari by changing your door. If your first choice is right, a switch will cost you the car. If it is wrong, the host, knowing where the car is, will reveal the other goat; and a switch will then win you the car. As your first choice had one way of being right and two ways of being wrong, the switch is definitely a good idea.

3

The Cave

Vision, in the sense of chapter 1, is a bold affair of vaulting to conclusions and science too goes partly by leaps. Reasoning, as described in chapter 2, is more a dogged business of small, justifying steps. So far, then, we are offered a high road of conjecture and a low road of argument. When they arrive at the same place, knowledge increases; and when they arrive at different places, conjecture is refuted. But often the low road does not stretch far enough for either verdict. That is no surprise, seeing that chapter 1 was largely about open questions and chapter 2 about closed ones. Yet it has also been my theme that there is no sharp boundary between them. The discovery of viruses closed open questions; the new power of computers is opening closed ones. The work of philosophy is at the shifting border between closed and open.

That makes paradox the very stuff of it. In the next six chapters I am going to assemble the paradox of free will as a collision between two excellent ways of thinking. One way belongs to our understanding of nature and the world which experience presents to us. The other suits our understanding of ourselves and the meaning which our experience has for us. Each makes a great deal of sense but they will not easily combine. The sense is not readily extracted, however, and each way of thinking is prone to paradoxes of its own. The next three chapters are about knowledge and why some robust, common-sensical stories of how the mind comes by its information will not do. In their place we shall try a story about knowledge as a web of belief. But that will not cure all headaches, we shall find. Then the following three will be about the self and morality in social life. Here it is all too plain that the pursuit of truth is not simple. The self which each of us is, or has, proves elusive. So does the basic knowledge of right and wrong, which we need to bring to our dealings with other people. Although I shall try to paint a philosophical portrait of human beings, it will be a perplexing one. But there will be enough of it to see why belief in free will is so stubborn and chapter 9 will explore various, infuriating attempts to square it with knowledge of the natural world, which human beings inhabit. The paradox, however, will remain as stubborn as the beliefs which generate it.

Two Worlds?

The starting point is the idea of knowledge and the blunt fact that we cannot climb out of our own heads. When you claim to know that there are elephants, you are saying something about the world and something about yourself. It needs to be true both that elephants exist and that you are warranted in believing it. The connection is supplied, sometimes anyway, by experience, which puts you in touch with the outside world and serves as evidence for your belief. Presumably, there are other ways of making the connection, since we all claim to know plenty which experience does not tell us directly or at all. (We do not experience the dinosaurs we believe to have existed, the huge prime numbers we believe to belong in the number series, the inner feelings of other people or the components of what we claim to be knowledge of right and wrong.) But our simplest knowledge is by contact between the mind and the world. Or so it is very plausible indeed to say. The trouble starts here.

Already that gives us two worlds, inner and outer. Elephants inhabit the outer and so, in one way or another, does much that exists independently of whether we believe it does. But not everything we are conscious of has an independent being. In some versions of the thought, the inner world is also furnished with objects, typified by the things which we see in dreams and including representations of real things (like tiny elephant-images, turned upside down in the process of perception?). But we need not take the blunt fact that we cannot climb out of our own heads so far. It is enough that experience has two aspects, one to do with the mind's experiencing and the other with what it warrants our believing in. That they are separate is clear, since they can come apart. Experience always tells us something but not always something true about the world.

There is a world outside our own heads but we cannot climb out and look at it. That thought makes assumptions which will need questioning later but meanwhile it raises a doubt – sceptical or mystical – about what the world is really like. I would like to begin with a very grand use of the doubt to suggest that experience is so human-centred that it reveals only shadows of reality. It comes from the fourth century BC and occurs at the point in Plato's *Republic* where Socrates compares mankind to prisoners in a cave. Sense experience, he suggests, cuts us off from the real truth of things, since our five senses present us only with 'shadows'. The *Republic* is in dialogue form and, at this moment, Socrates is conversing with his friend Glaucon. (This and the subsequent passage are from the translation by H.D.P. Lee, Penguin Books, 1955.)

'Imagine an underground chamber, like a cave with an entrance open to the daylight and running a long way underground. In this chamber are men who have been prisoners there since they were children, their legs and necks being so fastened that they can only look straight ahead of them and cannot turn their heads. Behind them and above them a fire is burning, and between the fire and the prisoners runs a road, in front of which a curtain-wall has been built, like the screen at puppet shows between the operators and their audience, above which they show their puppets.'

'I see.'

'Imagine further that there are men carrying all sorts of gear along behind the curtain-wall, including figures of men and animals made of wood and stone and other materials, and that some of these men, as is natural, are talking and some are not.'

'An odd picture and an odd sort of prisoner.'

'They are drawn from life,' I replied. 'For, tell me, do you think our

prisoners could see anything of themselves or their fellows except the
shadows thrown by the fire on the wall of the cave opposite them?'
'How could they see anything else if they were prevented from
moving their heads all their lives?'
'And would they see anything more of the objects carried along the
road?'
'Of course not.'
'Then if they were able to talk to each other, would they not assume
that the shadows they saw were real things?'
'Inevitably.'

As Glaucon says, the picture is indeed an odd one and you may
well ask whether we are truly like these prisoners. Unlike them, we
are surely in touch with things as often as with shadows and know
the difference. Or, if a modern Socrates were to present the prisoners
as television viewers, condemned only ever to see the screen and to
experience things only at second hand, you might well protest
similarly. But Socrates is adamant that experience of reality is possible
only for someone who escapes from the cave. If a prisoner were
taken up to the fire, he would see things as they are and he would
be too dazzled to make much of them at first. It would be even
worse, if he was forced into the sunlight. But, when he grew
accustomed to the light, he would realize that all his previous
experience was only of shadows.

The contrast drawn is less between things as we know them and
things as they are than between what we experience with the five
senses and what we can come to understand in another way. All the
same the upshot is a world which the senses cannot reach. Within
the world of shadows, the prisoners can try distinguishing between
the real and the merely apparent. For instance, some prisoners may
dream or hallucinate and thus have experiences which others do not
share. But 'real' in the shadows will not mean more than 'public' or
'confirmable by others'. It does not refer to what the mind, in the
person of the escaping prisoner, grasps directly by the light of the fire
or the sun.

Plato puts forward one of the earliest and most haunting of the

'two-world' theories but his is not the only one. Others range from
the overtly religious, with a second, supernatural world of angels or
devils or other spirits, to the hard-headedly scientific, whose second
world houses hidden forces like gravity or entities like quarks. This
is not the moment to explore Plato's own, interesting though it
remains. The point is that second-world theories share a belief in the
limits of (everyday or secular or human or finite) experience as a
guide to the true order of things. That lays them all open to an
objection: how could we possibly know? We can judge how good
a guide television pictures are to the world they inform us about,
because we can compare. But how can we possibly say anything
about a second world, if it is true that our experience confines us to
one?

Plato's answer is that the senses are not our only source of
experience. We also have an intellect and, once we set aside the
bodily concerns of our physical being, can use it to 'see' with. The
senses can tell us truly about shadows; the intellect about the causes
of shadows. Learning to use the intellect is hard, however, and risky:

> 'Then what do you think would happen,' I asked, 'if he went back
> to sit in his old seat in the cave? Wouldn't his eyes be blinded by the
> darkness, because he had come in suddenly out of the daylight?'
> 'Certainly.'
> 'And if he had to discriminate between the shadows, in competition
> with the other prisoners, while he was still blinded and before his eyes
> got used to the darkness – a process that might take some time –
> wouldn't he be likely to make a fool of himself? And they would say
> that his visit to the upper world had ruined his sight, and that the
> ascent was not worth even attempting. And if anyone tried to release
> them and lead them up, they would kill him if they could lay hands
> on him.'

Socrates was later condemned to death for 'subverting the youth'
with his philosophizing and was executed by drinking hemlock in
399 BC (as movingly recorded in Plato's dialogue *Phaedo*). No doubt
Plato had this in mind, when making the fruits of intellect bitter-

sweet. But the puzzle is not peculiar to Greek or any other culture. It needs only a tension between the world which the senses present and the world as we understand it to be. Practical persons often deny that there is any such tension, since they manage well enough with the world which they experience and cannot see the need for another. But I think there is a genuine tension, as I shall explain below.

Subjective and Objective

Touch a wet sponge and a message travels from your fingertips to your brain, where it is decoded. There is a causal chain with a sponge at one end and an experiencing at the other. When we speak of 'the experience of a sponge', it is not plain quite what is referred to but a long and plausible tradition has it that you infer the presence of a sponge from what you actually experience. One reason is that there is nothing unreal about the experiences had in dreams or hallucinations. What fails is the inference to the outside cause, not the premise it starts from. In that case it must be possible to describe an experience without pre-judging its causes; and the mind's contact, in sense perception, is with whatever can be so described. When there is a sponge to touch, the inference succeeds and, when there is not, it fails; but it starts from the same experience, whether it succeeds or not.

That sounds very like the cave in spirit, with 'shadows', in the form of subject-centred experiences, and 'reality' as the physical things, which cause them. It also sounds like an account of perception from a standard biology textbook. Yet it raises a question straightaway. How do we know about these physical things? The sponge, at least, seems easy. You feel it; you look and see it; other people can see and feel it too. But, on reflection, it is not so simple, if there is inference involved. The sponge, which you feel, you infer from one experience and the sponge, which you see, you infer from another sort of experience. To know that other people feel or see the sponge, you must infer that they have experiences like yours; and this inference is a daring leap into inner worlds, which you never experience at all. The claim that there really is a sponge in front of you rests unsteadily on a narrow set of your own experiences and some pious hopes about other people's. The sponge itself has slid mysteriously from your ken into a second world which you cannot get at.

Notice how enjoyably the ground crumbles under the solid steps of common sense. You start with the simple touching of a familiar object, realize that there is a subject-centred end to a chain of cause and effect and find that the sponge is only a conjecture. Plato's eccentric image of the cave is suddenly just right. That is very odd but here is one reason for putting up with it. The chapter on Reasoning discussed inference under the headings of 'Proof' and 'Evidence'. Which heading covers the inference from the experience to the sponge which caused it? It cannot be proof, if experiences can be described without implying that they have any particular (or even any) cause. If the same premise does for an argument whose conclusion is that you are hallucinating as for one which concludes that there is a sponge by your hand, and if both conclusions are possible, then logic does not guarantee that there are sponges. It does not take Plato's prisoners beyond the shadows.

So, presumably, the natural heading is 'Evidence'. Certainly, the experience of touching a wet sponge seems good evidence that there is a sponge there to touch. But evidence depends on analogy with similar cases. Disconcertingly, given the line taken in the last few pages, there are *no* cases, where a causal chain has been traced to its outer source. Since the source is in a world beyond the reach of experience, we have *no* experience to build on. That seems to follow from the blunt fact that we cannot climb out of our own heads.

Take the point more slowly. If the starter of your car has a habit of jamming, then, next time you switch on and hear the familiar dead clunk, you will infer that it has jammed again. Logic does not guarantee it but previous evidence supports the conclusion and, crucially, you can open the bonnet to check. This is an everyday example of tracing a causal chain to its source by means of an analogy with known cases. Contrast it with an analogy offered to show that today's thunderstorm is the result of ill temper by the god of thunder, since it is just like previous storms. This analogy suffers from having no previous cases to appeal to, as is hardly surprising, if the gods are held to dwell in a realm beyond our reach. A million storms are no evidence for a conclusion which can be checked for none of them. The upshot of confining experience to the receiving end of causal chains is that the solid world of physical things melts away and becomes a conjectured realm of gods.

I do not mean that we can never know the causes of experience. The fault in the starter motor has not suddenly become the work of leprechauns. But tracing the fault has become a matter of relating one experience to other experiences, rather than of locating it in a 'second world'. At any rate this is the conclusion which we shall reach, if we push the line of thought to the limit. From these three premises:

1   Only experience can justify claims to know what there is
2   'Experience' refers to subject-centred events and objects
3   Neither Proof nor Evidence warrants an inference from experience to what could not be experienced.

We get the conclusion that belief in a second world is unwarranted.

The conclusion is both tempting and odd. It is odd because it startles obvious common sense. Out of my window I can see houses, pylons and trees. They are solid and at a distance. They will still be there after dark, when I no longer see them. They are not subject-centred experiencings of mine but belong in an independent landscape. So does the wind, which moves the trees, although I experience only its effects. There is something downright peculiar about an argument which puts all this furniture on a par with hidden gods. Yet the argument began very much in tune with common sense. We believe in trees and not in leprechauns, because experience commands it. It is very tempting to hold that only experience supplies the warrants which justify our knowledge of reality. It is easy to accept that experience is subject-centred and operates at the receiving end of information. The simple rules given for proof and evidence are sensible. Yet, in tempting us to put our trust in experience, the argument lures common sense into a paradox.

How deep does the paradox go? The test is whether it can be resolved without upsetting the system which spawned it. Chapter 1 gave examples of merely mild paradoxes. Whether the satellite circled the Earth was a trivial question, granted that there are different meanings of 'to circle' (p.7). The vanishing philosopher on p.10 (figures 1 and 2) does not truly vanish – anyone, who describes what happens in a clear-headed way, will see that 15 old philosophers have been replaced with 14 new ones. It ceases to be paradoxical that better hygiene kills, as soon as the causal chains have been properly traced (p.11). Has anything yet been said about knowledge and experience, which a spot of clear thinking will not set straight?

Plato's answer would be that the paradox is genuine for anyone who tries to confine human knowledge to sense-experience and what it warrants. But it is too soon to abandon the claims of experience. So let us see whether we can sort them out more clearly. I have been inviting you to think of experience as 'subject-centred' for two different sorts of reason. One has to do with the mechanics of perception in a textbook story about how outside objects excite the nervous system and the brain or mind is at the receiving end. This seems to make it a matter of scientific fact that we are cut off from what common sense tells us we perceive all the time. The other concerns the human element of awareness, which goes into an experiencing. This (for further reasons, which we shall come to) tempts us into giving the mind a set of immediate, mental data to work on. I shall next suggest that paradoxes inspired by the first sort of reason are spurious but those provoked by the second go deep.

Even in the Cave, there need be nothing subjective about the shadows, just because they are not the objects which cause them. The prisoners can name, describe and discuss them. They can work out tests for when, for instance, a shadow-winejar has merely been dreamt by one prisoner and when it is real because publicly visible. In this sight-only world shadow-winejars work very much as solid winejars do in ours. They are not figments of the mind. Yet they are no less at the receiving end of the nervous system than are the trees and pylons, which I see from my window. If we can arrive at a two-world theory by considering the mechanics of perception, so can the prisoners in the cave, since the shadows will turn out not to be experienced either. A shadow-winejar is the inferred cause of the subject-centred experience of a shadow-winejar and there are the same snags to the inference. If the mechanics of perception turn trees into shadows, then they turn shadows into shadows of shadows.

These mechanics are not in themselves puzzling. Yet they would be, if so construed as to cut us off from physical things. Retinas in the eye, stirrup bones in the ear and synapses in the chain of nerves are physical things too. If biology casts radical doubt on common sense, then it also casts radical doubt on biology. We certainly cannot show that we never perceive physical things directly by citing evidence which assumes that we do! The same goes for the variant of the argument, which uses the very different physiology of insects to show that human knowledge of the world is by inference. A radical suggestion that flies see a different world with their thousand eyes is a radical doubt about our knowledge of flies. But the little word 'radical' is doing a lot of work. Flies get their news of the world differently from us and it is different news. We can know about them, however, only if we do not mean that they literally have news of a different world. That radical suggestion could not be a known scientific fact.

Knowledge and Belief

The element of awareness in experience is, alas, much more paradoxical. Notions of objectivity, which require the mind to be self-effacing, clash with notions of consciousness, which make self-effacement impossible. 'Experience', as I have been using the word, tries to combine object and interpretation. The blending is unstable so far, I think. Let us turn to the notion of objectivity, taking photography as a starting point. The camera records what is in front of it: it never lies. If the cliché produces a hollow laugh, that is not the fault of the camera. Misleading images are the work of people – the viewer as often as the photographer – not of the film passively registering a scene from a perspective. But 'objectivity' here refers not to the record on the film but to the result of correcting for perspective. It is about how things objectively were when the shutter moved. It must eliminate both perspective and human error; and it needs an active mind to achieve it. We still cannot climb out of our own heads.

Any paradox involved is not special to perception but general for all knowledge, construed as a relation of mind to object. Thus, by one famous analysis, knowledge is *justified, true belief*, inasmuch as you know that something is the case only if:

1   you believe it
2   you are correct
3   you have sufficient warrant.

(These conditions are not in fact sufficient. For example, if you do not know that your reliable old clock has stopped exactly 12 hours ago, you hold a true and justified belief that it shows the right time. But, since you would hold the same belief, had it stopped 11 hours ago, you do not *know* the right time. The conditions do, however, cover enough of the ground for present purposes.) The analysis requires the mind to check belief against reality, as if such self-effacement were possible. The same goes for analyses which try replacing the third condition with one to the effect that the belief must be caused by reality in a suitable way. How, one wonders, do we have independent access to reality? But that is to run ahead of my theme. To avoid confusion, let us return firmly to the proposition that knowledge is justified, true belief and take it more slowly.

The conditions apply equally to, for instance, geometry. To know that all triangles with sides of 3 cm, 4 cm and 5 cm are right-angled, it must be true, you must believe it true and you must have some warrant, like a proof involving Pythagoras' theorem, for believing it. The warrant clause leaves it open what kind and strength of warrant is proper for what sort of case. But it has to be there to rule out, for example, guesswork. When you guess the weight of the cake at the fête, you may be right but you do not know the weight. When you hate someone so much that you believe the worst of him without weighing the evidence, your belief may be true but it is not justified.

Conversely, you may have a strong warrant for a belief which is false. When people believed the Earth to be flat, they had pretty good reasons. Simple experience suggested that it was flat and the authority of men of learning said the same. But no one *knew* it was flat, for the decisive reason that it isn't. Hence it is, in general, one question whether a belief is justified and another whether it is true. On reflection, however, that is by no means a plain and harmless distinction. Like people in the Middle Ages, we too have a body of beliefs, backed by experience and authority, which we take to satisfy the 'truth' condition. Like them, we claim an objectivity gained by correcting for what is subject-centred. Can we be sure that we *know* more than they?

The question has its harmless side. No doubt future ages will think us foolish and ignorant. That need not worry us. Like the medievals, we fare well enough with our system of beliefs to be sure that it is basically in order. Besides, for us the authority of learning is less bound up with religion and makes a virtue of being open to correction. Admittedly, it would be shattering to find that the Earth was flat after all. But that is because we would have to scrap so much of our optics, astronomy, physics and other science that the idea is close to inconceivable for us. On the other hand, there is no worry about our proving to have been wrong in ways which leave our basic map undisturbed. Our self-esteem is not threatened by the idea that future ages will have better information.

Descartes and the Demon

In the smug confidence that most of what we take for knowledge is truly knowledge, we deny being prisoners of our concepts and beliefs. Yet, in granting that the medievals had 'pretty good reasons' for believing the world to be flat, we think them the prisoners of theirs. In part, admittedly, they had good reasons because they were confined to a smaller information base than we. But knowledge involves more than information. It needs a framework and the medievals had a powerful, well-integrated one. In speaking of their 'good reasons', we are using the term in a sense not demanding that their framework is right. We mean, roughly, that the belief fitted neatly into a scheme of beliefs which gave experience shape and significance. Can we say more than that about our own justified beliefs? It is hard to see how. But, if not, then to justify a belief is to connect it to those already accepted and not to match it to reality. The truth condition, by being distinct from the good-reasons clause, threatens to turn objectivity into a will-o'-the-wisp.

This is why it is awkward that we cannot climb out of our own heads: we cannot climb out of our systems of beliefs. Yet we try, and I want next to introduce some arguments from the most influential recent attempt. Their source is René Descartes, the seventeenth-century philosopher and scientist, whose *Meditations on First Philosophy* (1641) opened our own intellectual world. In his time, and for at least a century, his work in mathematics and physics vied with Sir Isaac Newton's as a commanding offer to make sense of what science had lately brought to light. Newton's theories finally displaced his but the *Meditations* remain fertile for anyone trying to understand the nature of knowledge in a philosophical way.

In the *Meditations*, Descartes set himself to ground modern science on simple truths, which anyone could grasp who had an unclouded mind. The aim was partly to secure a scientific method free of preconceptions and partly to show that the new science was no threat to religion. It needed something drastic, as he explained at the start of the book:

It is now some years since I detected how many were the false beliefs that I had from my earliest youth admitted as true, and how doubtful was everything I had since constructed on this basis; and from that time I was convinced that I must once and for all seriously undertake to rid myself of the opinions which I had formerly accepted, and commence to build anew from the foundation, if I wanted to establish any firm and permanent structures in the sciences.

This purge of old opinions was to be conducted by a 'method of doubt'. He proceeded to work through each kind of belief which he held, issuing a challenge to their truth and suspending judgement until the challenge could be met. For, he explained elsewhere, if you have a barrel of apples and need to find the bad ones without fail, you must empty out all the apples, check them one by one and put only good ones back. The test was to be very searching. He began with the beliefs which he had acquired by relying on his five senses. Mistakes, he argued, certainly occur, most obviously when I dream of something, which turns out not to be real. There are common sense checks for detecting dreams and illusions but they all depend on an inconsistency between one lot of perceptions and another. For instance, I know that I was only dreaming a moment ago because those experiences are not supported by my present ones. A madman's perceptions are vivid enough to him but do not fit with other people's. In that case, however, common sense checks do not truly answer a challenge to the five senses. They fail to establish that what we call waking experience is not part of a larger and more coherent dream. 'How often has it happened to me that in the night I dreamt that I found myself in this particular place, that I was dressed and seated by the fire, whilst in reality I was lying undressed in bed!' Perhaps 'in reality' even the experience of waking up in bed belongs to some larger dream.

Once this doubt is taken seriously, it is not to be settled by pointing out how solid is the bulk of our experiences. Pinching oneself does not prove one is awake! In a compelling image Descartes goes on to suppose that 'some evil genius has employed his whole energies in deceiving me'. This malignant demon is causing me to experience 'the heavens, the earth, colours, figures and sounds', when in truth I have 'no hands, no eyes, no flesh, no blood nor any senses, yet falsely believing myself to possess all these things'. Or, to borrow an image from twentieth-century science fiction, perhaps I am only a brain suspended in a vat in a laboratory, wired up and programmed so that my experience is just as it is. Until I can refute this hypothesis, I cannot trust my senses ever to inform me about what there is.

The point is not that we are really brains in a vat nor even that we seriously might be. It is that the senses cannot issue their own guarantee of accuracy. We need a warrant to trust them and the warrant must come from elsewhere. Without the warrant we cannot judge even that the malignant demon is an unlikely hypothesis, since, as we have seen, all evidence relies on known cases. Descartes has found a graphic way of pointing out that a two-world theory is not going to be able to establish the existence of a second world on the evidence of the senses. So, he continues, I need a bedrock – something which not even an evil genius could fool a brain in a vat about.

That something turns out to be Descartes' own existence. Strictly it is not even the existence of his brain, since a brain is a physical thing and so could, in theory, be dreamt up. It is the mind or self. The most cunning demon could not fool Descartes into believing falsely that Descartes exists: if there is no Descartes, there is nothing to fool. So, for each of us, the self is bedrock and Descartes reaches it with three famous Latin words, *cogito ergo sum*, 'I think, therefore I am.' (The bedrock is not granite pure and simple. Descartes remarks elsewhere that '*ergo*' is misleading, because I do not infer my existence but intuit it. Also 'I think' is a questionable translation of '*cogito*' and the clumsier 'I am having conscious experiences' may be better. So might 'I exist' for '*sum*'. But 'I think, therefore I am' is a famous tag and accurate enough for what follows.)

What am I? A something, a substance, a being whose essence is its consciousness, a mental and not a physical unit. Very well, but how does that help with the warrant for my belief in the physical world? How does it refute the demon hypothesis? In itself, it does not. But, reflecting on how I recognized bedrock, I see that I have a principle to work with – that whatever I clearly and distinctly conceive is true. Reflecting further, I find that I clearly and distinctly conceive of God, a supreme being who is no deceiver. A good God will have created us with the ability to understand his creation and the way is clear for further understanding of the world about me, of my place in it and my own nature. (The exact order of all these steps is a matter of scholarly dispute.) That is very broadly how Descartes hoped to ground the mathematical principles of his new physics and guide his readers to grasp the most basic truths about them, the world and human nature through an openness to God. It is also why he could maintain, strangely to the modern ear, that atheists could not fully master science.

These fleeting remarks do no more than hint at his sweeping ambitions and the sharp, elegant arguments which he brought to bear. Their purpose is to illustrate something different, the place of abstract, seemingly contrived reasoning in practical affairs. (I count religion as practical, along with science and common sense; there is nothing more practical than discovering how we ought to live.) Take, for instance, the suggestion that you may merely be dreaming that you are reading this chapter. It seems a queer start to meditations on God, nature and human existence. Yet, if one settles down to it in the right frame of mind, it is very instructive.

The historical context of the *Meditations* means that the stakes are higher than a modern reader might guess from the apparently quaint and amiable text. At the time our modern scientific world was only starting to take shape, as the telescope and other instruments yielded unsettling news. The news seemed to be that the traditional picture of nature was rich in sheer fabrication. Bluntly, nature was not as the Bible, interpreted by the Church and taught with ecclesiastical approval in schools, declared it to be. Thanks to men like Descartes and Newton, it was proving to be a system of forces or mass in motion. It was emerging as a machine or perfect clockwork, whose workings obeyed principles of mechanics and mathematics. This was as disturbing to religious people of the time (and that meant almost everyone) as is the threat to our own cherished beliefs about ourselves, which recent work on computers and artificial intelligence brings today. Consequently, Descartes' sense that he had been reared on a tissue of false belief was an urgent one. His faith in a God, who was somehow author of all, was undisturbed but there was a need to restate the basis of scientific knowledge without the help of its traditional authority.

How might one focus so grand a project? It needs a question small and precise enough to be manageable, yet promising large implications. So let us probe the difference between dreaming and waking experience, to see if that is the key to larger questions about appearance and reality. The results are liable to surprise us. We find that we commonly construe experience in a way which is subject-centred but construe the pointers to reality, which experience gives us, in a way which is not. Experience threatens to emerge as more of a gaoler than a guide. This becomes plain when we try to refute the fancy that an evil genius has staged all our experience with intent to fool us into coherent yet false beliefs. If we conclude that experience is, so to speak, printing its own money, then, like Descartes, we need some authority outside it.

This is the grand purpose of the small question about waking and dreaming. But it does not mean that the question has been well posed. Later argument about perception, what the senses present to us and how their direct information relates to reality, has been fierce and subtle. It continues unabated in epistemology and also troubles the philosophy of mind. Some main lines are sketched in the next chapters. First let me take stock by returning to the cave.

Conclusion

Plato speaks of firelight and of sunlight. The shadows are cast by firelight falling on the objects which cause them. That is a metaphor for a knowledge of the world, which the senses do not give. We have found one good and one doubtful reason to take the metaphor seriously. The doubtful one is the fact that we find it natural to regard sense experience as a link between inner and outer worlds. The feel of a damp sponge is information at the receiving end of a causal chain, it seems, with the sponge 'out there' at the other end. But this cannot be quite what we learn from human anatomy since, in that case, our anatomy is 'out there' too. All the same, there is some distinction between experiences and objects, as we saw with Descartes' dreams. But it has more to do with the good reason for some kind of two-world theory, the fact that the mind cannot be wholly self-effacing. This will be a main topic of the next chapter.

Plato's 'sunlight' is a metaphor for a bolder claim that the order of things — the true moral order of the universe — can be understood only by a mind spiritually and intellectually attuned to it. This ideal understanding has been a recurrent theme among the boldest philosophers and theologians. At the same time, however, philosophers of hard-headed tendency have always refused to put the slightest faith in it. I mention it as an example of Vision, to remind us that philosophy can be played for very high stakes indeed. Meanwhile, there is enough to think about in the idea that knowledge is what we see by firelight and not just the shadows in the Cave.

4
Ants, Spiders and Bees

Every thinking person has beliefs about the furniture of heaven and earth. These range from an everyday certainty that the world contains chairs, tables and other people to a reflective trust in the electrons of physics or the gods of religion. Even within a single culture beliefs vary and between cultures or periods of history they vary enormously. Examples of disputed furniture which spring to mind are witches, tree spirits, angels and other hidden agencies. But Western science is as good a source, witness the crystal spheres once thought to ring the Earth, the *homunculi* or complete miniature people which human ova were once held to contain or the ether once believed to fill the gaps between celestial bodies. Nor is dispute confined to the past – think of rival theories about particles in physics, or about human motivation in economics or psychiatry. Taking a broad compass, we can add that even 'common sense' is not the same everywhere.

A good response to this variety is, like Descartes, to look for a test of truth, which can help detect false or unwarranted beliefs. That is not plain sailing. The last chapter tried a test in terms of experience, backed up by proof and evidence, and seemed to get the odd result that it was hard to justify even belief in tables and chairs. Nothing yet follows, of course, about tables and chairs. A favourite among graffiti runs, 'Do not adjust your set: there is a fault in reality.' Perhaps there is; but we would do well to start by checking the set. In this chapter I shall be considering some ways of cashing in Plato's metaphor of 'firelight' for knowledge of reality, starting with a defence of the claims of experience against the stringent sort of method of doubt which Descartes proposed.

The insects of the chapter's title comes from another seventeenth-century thinker, Sir Francis Bacon, whose pithy reflections on scientific method are still widely heeded. In his *First Book of Aphorisms* (1625) he remarks, 'Those who have handled the sciences have been either men of experiment or men of dogmas. The men of experiment are like the ant, they only collect and use; the reasoners resemble spiders, who make cobwebs out of their substance.' Despite his dismissive tone, however, he see some virtue in both and goes on to recommend 'a middle way', symbolized by the bee, which 'gathers material from the flowers of the garden and of the field but transforms and digests it by a power of its own.' In plainer words, there have been two common tendencies in the theory of knowledge. One is to rely on experience and the senses; the other to rely on the kind of reasoning and model-making typical of mathematics. Bacon would have us combine the two; but it will not prove easy to oblige.

Foundations of Knowledge

Egged on by Descartes' demon, we began with the experience of feeling a sponge and were unable to justify the belief that there was a sponge there. The sponge was a matter of inference and neither proof nor evidence could serve. You may well object to this paradoxical result. When conjured up without warning, it is, to say the least, strange. But there is a classic reason for taking it seriously, connected with the point that inference adds to knowledge, only if its premises are known truths. A proof shows that, if x is so, then y is also so. Evidence shows that, given x, y is (probably) so. Both need an x to start from. Experience provided one only if it could be described independently of physical objects. But, even allowing that dreaming is experience without physical objects, do we really want to detach the sponge in this odd way? The classic reason for saying 'Yes' is that there needs to be an x somewhere in the story, which requires neither proof nor evidence. Here is a classic supporting argument.

Suppose that you were to list every belief which you hold and settle down to weed out any which you are not warranted in holding. Sometimes you will decide that a belief is, on reflection, false. More often, however, you will have to suspend judgement, because one entry on the list depends on the truth of others. So suppose you put a star against any entry which must wait. Now suppose you find a ring of stars, where belief *a* depends on belief *b*, which depends on belief *c*, which depends on . . . belief *a* again. Here, it is very plausible to rule, the whole ring should be rejected. At any rate that is what we decide about beliefs in, for instance, fairies or witches. It does not matter how large the ring is. If you cannot establish *a* by reference to *b*, while also resting *b* on *a*, then you cannot work the same trick with a thousand beliefs in a ring. In that case, when your task is done, you need to be left with some beliefs which have no star but which you know to be true. Knowledge relies ultimately on some truths, known without proof or evidence.

We glimpsed this old and crucial line of thought at work in Descartes' *Meditations*, where it resulted in his famous *cogito* ('I think, therefore I am'). Its upshot is that there must be foundations of knowledge. (Whether or not Descartes found the true ones is another matter.) It is a very persuasive line of thought and, at least until lately, has been the accepted starting point for accounts of human knowledge. In its abstract form, however, it gives no hint what the truths are, which we know without proof or evidence. That is where the dispute comes. In fact there have been many disputes, since the abstract case applies equally to, say, ethics or religion, where it leads on questions about knowledge from conscience or revelation. But I want to concentrate on the basis of science and everyday common sense, which brings us back to Francis Bacon.

Bacon's contrast between men of dogmas (the spiders) and men of experiment (the ants) is pointed up by another remark from his *First Book of Aphorisms*:

There are and can only be two ways of searching into and discovering truth. The one flies from senses and particulars to the most general axioms and from these, the truth of which it takes for settled and immovable, proceeds to judgement and middle axioms . . . The other derives axioms from the senses and particulars, rising by a gradual and unbroken ascent, so that it arrives at the most general axioms last of all.

There are, as he says, two especially tempting ways to turn. Many thinkers have tried, in the spirit of Bacon's bees, to combine them but I shall start by taking them separately.

The way which 'flies from the senses' is best seen in mathematics. Its attraction is that proof in mathematics leaves no room for doubt. For instance, no one who grasps simple arithmetic can doubt that 13 × 13 = 169. If the two shorter sides of a right-angled triangle are 3 cms and 4 cms, the third side is an indisputable 5 cms; it is not roughly 5 cms or usually 5 cms but a simple, inescapable 5 cms precisely. Why exactly is there no room for doubt? One reason is the compelling clarity of Pythagoras' theorem, implying that the sides a, b, c of any right-angled triangle stand in the relation $a^2 + b^2 = c^2$. The proof sets off from simple axioms and goes by clear steps. Without it, it is not at all obvious that a triangle with sides of 3 cms and 4 cms meeting at right angles has a third side of 5 cms. Once seen, however, it becomes part of our knowledge. Here is a tempting model for knowledge as a system grounded on axioms. A further reason, which removes doubt, is a notable feature of mathematical truths, the fact that they not only *are* true but also *must* be true and *could not* be false. This echoes the distinction in chapter 2 between statements whose falsity is impossible and those whose falsity is merely improbable. Here is a promising model for knowledge as truth beyond all possible doubt.

Combining these features, we catch the vision which 'spiders' have had, in a tradition going back to Plato's cave. Reality is masked by appearance and is not presented to our five senses. But the intellect can penetrate to the true order of things, as is done when a physicist uses mathematics. The test of truth is the guarantee that what mathematics shows with utter clarity could not possibly be otherwise. I stress the word 'vision'. It makes complete sense only if our experience is prompted by a hidden, fully ordered universe as perfect and immovable as in a physicist's pure abstractions. In that case there is no deep truth in the senses and we should fly to absolute principles which all matter obeys. Mathematics becomes our best example of how to satisfy the conditions, which the purest knowledge demands. But the step from the success of mathematics in extending our grasp of physics to a whole universe, which is somehow of the same character, is a wild leap in the dark. How daring is the spider's vision becomes plain as we turn to the ant.

Bacon suspects that the men of dogmas, who share this vision, spin cobwebs out of their own substance. His own view is that we should derive our axioms from the senses. The modern term for theories of knowledge which base themselves on experience supplied by the senses is 'empiricist' and the word has a practical, down-to-earth flavour even in everyday use. So we might expect that the 'men of experiment' stand closer to common sense. But that is not altogether true. Modern empiricism arose historically in answer to the 'men of dogmas' (usually termed rationalists) and shared some crucial seventeenth-century assumptions. Empiricists too accepted not only the need for foundations of knowledge but also that the foundations had to be beyond doubt. For, even with a foundation in experience, there is still the plausible thought that what is not beyond doubt needs justifying further. That leads to an early break with common sense.

It has led, in fact, to foundations which are, somehow, subjective. When you claim to see, say, an elephant, you commit yourself to more than is obvious at once. For instance, a genuine elephant, as opposed to cardboard cutouts, elephants in dreams and drunkards' elephants, is a solid creature, with typical near sides, far sides, outsides and insides. It existed a moment ago and will be somewhere a moment hence. It has (at least most of) the powers and habits of others of its kind. Other people can perceive it too. Returning to the business of listing all your beliefs and starring those which depend on the truth of others, you should, it seems, put a star against the belief that you see an elephant. For, were these commitments to fail you, it would not be true that you see a genuine one. Yet your original experience would be unchanged. It would still have been a genuine experience. Hence there is a more neutral description of the experience, which captures its content without giving hostages and which does not have to be treated as starred. Since it involves no risks, it needs no further justifying. By that token, however, it describes an experience private to you. Or so runs the classic line.

There are several aspects to this privacy, arising from the several ways in which risk is avoided. You take a risk, if you depend on what anyone else would say, now or later, about what is present to your senses. You take a risk even by claiming that you now perceive what you remember perceiving a moment ago. 'Private' refers to domain of your own consciousness and the experience which occupies it for this fragment of time. You, and no one else, have a direct, privileged access and that fact is what lets sense experience serve as a foundation of knowledge. Experience presents each of us with private, momentary atoms of consciousness and all other knowledge of the world is erected on this modest base.

Common sense starts with nothing so fine-grained. It deals in solid objects in an outside world, which has lasted for ages and is likely to continue much the same. But a fine-grained empiricism is not worried on that score, since it intends to treat the atoms of consciousness as the micro-foundations of the everyday macro-world. Experiences, although private, are orderly. Yours let you predict from one to another; so do mine; and we can pool our predictions with success. Thus you know and I know and we know that what looks like an elephant will probably lumber away, if there is a gunshot. By applying the rules of evidence to the regularities, which we find in experience, we can go on to describe the world in the terms of common sense and yet in a way which helps the advance of science. For, when common sense and science differ, for instance about whether the sun is larger than the earth, there is a test of truth by making predictions and seeing which are upheld. That is why

Bacon calls those who favour this sort of approach 'men of experiment'.

The version which I have just sketched was known in the seventeenth century as 'the way of ideas'. The very name helps to bring out why it is not really common-sensical. 'Ideas' meant any experience in consciousness (not merely thoughts or concepts, as in modern usage) and the 'way' was supposed to lead from the inner world of the mind to the world of nature which caused ideas in us. The mind, said John Locke in his *Essay Concerning Human Understanding* (1690) starts as 'white paper, void of all characters, without any ideas' and nature writes on the blank paper whatever we come to know about the world outside. There is, however, the huge snag, which we have met already, when talking about two-world theories. If the starting point is in a world of private, momentary, mental atoms, then the rules of evidence will not let us advance to knowledge of a world of public, lasting, physical things. That would require somehow climbing out of our own heads to compare experience with object in some cases, in order to find the regularities which cover others. I cannot climb out of my own head; and still less can I climb into yours, in order to calibrate our pooled account. It seems that a way of ideas, which starts with ideas, can never get beyond them.

This is only a snag, if there is a need for a second world. Certainly we are wedded to a language of chairs and tables, planets and particles. But empiricists of the fine-grained sort have not been downcast. If the language of macroscopic objects is a species of shorthand for much longer statements about the micro-world of experience, then we can happily both think with the mind of science and speak with the tongue of common sense. Whether this offers a successful way of treating the relation of reality and experience is a very hard question, still very much alive and, in one form or another, giving rise to immense industry. I shall not try to pass judgement. Instead let us note how neat an account of scientific method we get by working solely with the one world which experience presents to us.

It is an account in keeping with figure 4 (p.42), which pictures science advancing, as it learns to refine its theories through the success and failure of prediction. Nature presents us with countless patterns, some spurious, some to be trusted. Spurious patterns are those which have held often enough to be interesting but which collapse on further enquiry. For example, all sorts of cures for cancer have looked promising at one time or another but none has held up. Genuine patterns are those which indeed hold, whenever the right conditions occur. Scientific method is a set of rules for telling the genuine from the spurious. The detail of the rules is very complex, witness any guide to statistics, but it sums up as a broad strategy like the percolator diagram. The percolator is simple at heart because it relies on one single test of truth, the success or failure of prediction.

'The men of experiment are like the ant,' said Bacon, 'they only collect and use'. Yet philosophically the ant is very neat: knowledge of the world needs foundations; they are there in the data of the five senses; we collect and use data to make hypotheses; we predict from the hypotheses and accept the verdict of further experience; we generalize our successes into true scientific theories. That seems an admirable way to 'derive axioms from the senses and particulars, rising by a gradual and unbroken ascent, so that it arrives at the most general axioms last of all'.

The Middle Way

So why prefer the bee, which 'gathers material from the flowers of the garden and field but transforms it by a power of its own'? The ant is too simple-minded, I think, even granting that very complex techniques and statistics are involved in making predictions. As we began to notice in chapter 2, there is more than predictive successes to telling genuine patterns from spurious ones. Somehow we must explain the pattern, find the cause or reason for it. At any rate that is the spider's ambition with what Bacon rudely calls cobwebs. We have looked at an attempt to treat experience as the impact of nature, described in mathematical physics, on subjective consciousness. Whatever the snags, it is strong on causes and reasons why. Explanation lies with laws of nature, which underlie experience, and prediction is justified only when it cottons on to them.

The ant objects that a second world is a fiction, which we can manage without. Certainly a world beyond experience, proof and evidence sounds like a fiction. But, at heart, the ant is objecting more broadly that there is flatly *no* order in nature of the kind proposed. 'Nature' is only what we can experience – a world not of hidden forces and iron laws but of patterns which happen to be stable and 'laws' which summarize the more useful ones. That is the perennial dispute between reason and experience in starkest form. The buzz from the bee is that both parties (rationalists and empiricists) are wrong. The mind does not somehow see beyond the senses but it has its own contribution to make to all knowledge.

We have already noted ways in which the mind contributes. It supplies the concepts for organizing experience and it makes the conjectures which take us beyond present evidence. Since there are always infinitely many patterns with some support in experience, it must depend partly on us which we pick out and how we project them. (Does the colour of gills affect the courtship of fish? That depends partly on how *we* anatomize colour. Don't tell the fish!) But, so far, this is not a very startling point, as it merely makes a place for imagination in the work of discovering truths. The startling idea is that knowledge, in the sense of a stock of justified, true, beliefs, has an element of ourselves in it. That is what Bacon meant by giving the mind 'a power of its own'.

Anyone who sets off in empiricist style down the Way of Ideas is soon inclined to agree. The path starts with subjective fragments of experience and advances to the common sense world of solid bodies (including the bodies of other observers), laid out in space and over time. Somehow the stuff from the flowers of the garden has been transformed into the furniture of heaven and earth. It has not, it seems, been done by the use of proof and evidence. Even the humble claim that there are elephants involves more than the pure experience typically used to justify it; and the claim that other observers have a consciousness like mine is beyond evidence, as so far construed. Somehow experience has been organized by bringing it under concepts, which classify the data of consciousness into objects. I say 'somehow' because there is a jump involved, very like the jump which we deem the ancient Greeks to have made, when they read their everyday experience as evidence of gods. That is not to call the concepts of our scheme of things unjustified but it is to suggest that we transform the material by a power of the mind. There is no gradual and unbroken ascent from the senses alone.

The mind's power, then, is to make sense of experience in terms which experience alone cannot justify. Take, for instance, the concepts of space and time. As heirs of Sir Isaac Newton, we think of space as a sort of infinite, invisible grid in which each body in the universe has a unique place at each moment, and of time as the unique series of these boxes. 'Unique' is a strong word. It requires that a grid-reference of three space- and one time-coordinates picks out at most one body. Two things *cannot* be in the same place at once. It requires also that any two events or states belong to the same single time-series, thus ruling out much of what science fiction writers try to imagine about possible worlds. Meanwhile the space-grid has exactly three dimensions and the time-series goes only forwards and at a uniform rate. I do not pretend to understand exactly how Einstein's theory of relativity has modified Newton's theory of absolute space and absolute time. But I am told that they combine into an absolute space-time (although changing the idea of position within it). At any rate we laymen are still broadly Newtonian and that is enough for the point which I wish to make.

The point is that our thinking about space and time involves necessities. There *must* be three space- and one time-dimensions; two things *cannot* be in the same place at once. Necessities are also involved in our thinking about causal laws, for instance in our insistence that a cause *cannot* occur later than its effect and *could not* fail to produce its effect in given conditions. Even my remarks about sponges and elephants have implicitly been assuming that physical objects *must* have various properties and *cannot* have others. What justifies our thinking in these absolute terms? It is not experience, granted that the senses tell us at most only what *is*, *was*, perhaps *will be* or *is always*. So the ant replies that nothing justifies the talk of necessities, since things never *must be* as they are (at least if we are discussing real features of the world and not merely the words we have chosen to define as we do). The spider replies that the necessities are 'out there' in the being of things and we know it by the use of intellect. The bee tries for a middle way.

The middle way is to reject the assumption of both the others that the knowing mind is passive. In knowing we do not just register the sponge or contemplate what Bertrand Russell once called 'the gelid peaks of pure mathematics'. We actively judge that a sponge is at our fingertips or Pythagoras' theorem is true. The difference is between what the mind is confronted with and what it achieves.

The idea of active judgement, as opposed to passive recording, ties together some points loosely made in chapter 2. It connects with a distinction there (pp.44–5) between map-making and model-building. Map-makers are trying to reproduce a landscape faithfully and, even if they have not yet seen all of it, the test is straightforwardly whether it is as they suggest. The model-builder sets out to capture the principles by which something works and the test is equivalence of output. For instance, the merits of modelling atoms as dancers on a ballroom floor may not be great but they do not depend on whether atoms literally resemble dancers. The merits of representing the kingfisher's power to allow for the refraction of light, when diving for fish, by a system of differential equations do not depend on whether the kingfisher could pass an examination in mathematics. A map must be one-to-one, whereas a model need only be 'as if' correct.

This picks up a loose end in figure 4. The figure has a mysterious fork where a hypothesis, which fails to square with the facts, must be either rejected or amended. Nothing was said about how the choice was to be made. It is not a choice dictated by the facts. We can now see the point of calling it a matter of judgement. The question has become one of, for example, the elegance and economy of the model, which the scientist is seeking to impose on the data of experience. The choice involves judging the value of the model and, if, for instance, its simplifying power is great enough, making amendments for the sake of keeping it.

That also links with the point that, in the testing of hypotheses against experience, the general propositions of a scientific theory are not exactly at risk. The example was that a failure of the demand for gin and whisky to respond to a selective tax change would not disturb the laws of supply and demand. That is, once again, because theories are not directly at the mercy of experience. There is also a matter of judgement in deciding how to respond to facts which refuse to fit the theory. There is, at least up to a point, always a further explanation or amendment and, in some important sense, the choice is ours.

A paradox threatened earlier because of the subject-centredness of our understanding. Knowledge demanded that we be self-effacing: yet we cannot climb out of our own heads. The element of active judgement in knowledge seems to resolve the paradox. Or does it? One small word has got lost in the last few pages – truth. There are all sorts of ways of conjuring an elegant theory out of thin air. For instance, cultures which believe deeply in witches and witchcraft are often very orderly in their thinking. They explain everyday mishaps as the work of witches in a connected manner, which makes detailed sense of many sorts of experience. There is plenty of active judgement going on. But the question remains whether they judge truly. Models can have all kinds of virtues and yet be false models. Concepts may have great organizing power and be the wrong concepts. So what becomes of truth, if we try for the middle way?

The answer which beckons is that there is only one finally consistent set of concepts and only one finally coherent scheme for organizing experience. So, although we *impose* the concepts of 'object', 'causal law', 'space' and 'time' on experience, we do not *choose* them from a list of alternatives. There is, indeed, a necessity about the space-time grid or the uniform, forward passage of time but it arises because there is no other way to give experience an objective framework. This answer is given most famously in Immanuel Kant's *The Critique of Pure Reason* (1781), which many regard as the most profound study yet written of the relation of reason to experience. It is also a very difficult work and I do not have the nerve to boil it down here. So, frustratingly, this is as far as I can take the discussion now. In a blunt sentence, the middle way would succeed, if active judgement has its guarantee of truth, because it imposes the only possible categories on experience. (This is not meant to rule out a different, more flexible test of success for the middle way, as will become plain in the next chapter.)

The question of truth can be put less grandly as one about knowledge and imagination. I said before that not even the ant objects to imagination as an aid to fertile hypotheses and to novel predictions; but that knowledge is concerned with justifying claims to truth. For instance, it helps in thinking about time, if we imagine what it would be like to travel in time. Dr Who, British television's roaming time-traveller, will do nicely, especially when he returns to the past to save Earth from aliens. Imagination wonders whether he will succeed; but, of course, he has to, because otherwise history would not be as we know it. The history books may perhaps have failed to record the Doctor's part in the Battle of Hastings in 1066, but in that case they have been incomplete ever since 1066. If he was there, then it makes no odds in what future year he steps aboard his time machine. He cannot return to *change* a year, whose complete history already includes whatever he did in it.

Still more plainly, he cannot intervene to change his own life. Just as he cannot prevent his own birth, so too he cannot change the socks which he wore on his tenth birthday. Indeed it is at best doubtful whether he can attend his tenth birthday party aged 203. For, although the complete guest list perhaps already contains a hitherto unrecorded stranger who claimed to be 203, he cannot be the same person as the 10-year-old birthday boy. Dr *Who*? is the right name for the mysterious stranger! The fancy makes no sense by our current rules of thought about time. It either shows us something interesting about time or demands a very radical revision of our ideas. The moral, either way, is that the discoveries made are only those which reason finally certifies.

The bee's middle way is that thoughts like these enrich not our knowledge of time as a feature of the universe but our knowledge of how we must conceive of time. The mind is discovering the mind. The middle way is precarious. It offends both common sense and scientific ambition. Common sense still objects to a notion of experience so tied to the data of the senses that even tables and chairs are a matter of gluing scattered data together with mere concepts. Science still wants the order of things, causes and forces 'out there' in space-time and not lodged merely in the cast of our minds. There is bound to be a suspicion that a false step has been taken. Either experience is more solid and in touch with the world or reason has a power to reveal truth about reality after all. In the end I shall leave it to you to decide which, if either, is the promising trail. But we have not finished with the middle way, as a brisk summary will show.

Conclusion

The chapter set off with a classic argument to show that knowledge needs 'foundations', in the sense of bedrock truths which we know without proof or evidence and which are beyond all doubt. The spiders or 'men of dogmas' found bedrock in simple truths, like the axioms of logic or mathematics, which have a necessity defying all doubt. The ants or 'men of experiment' relied on the very simplest sense-impressions and built on those by inference. Both parties, however, were assuming that, when it knows, the unclouded and attentive mind is passively accepting a truth. But can the mind possibly efface itself to this degree? The middle way made a virtue of saying 'No'. It replaced passive recording with active judgement. But that left a worry about truth, which I do not suppose that I have removed. Perhaps the worry would change shape, if the very first move was a mistake. Does knowledge really need 'foundations'? Many philosophers lately have come to deny it and the next task is to see whether they are right.

5

The Web of Belief

The bee gathers its material from the flowers of the field and digests it by a power of its own. This allegory of the mind at work can be attacked from opposite sides. The bluntest objection comes from a common sense, which refuses to be puzzled by perception. The plain common sense fact is that we are surrounded by solid, physical objects, which we know to be there because we perceive them. So what possible merit can there be in a theory of the mind, which turns this basic and obvious fact into a matter of daring and fragile inference? I shall start by trying to head off this frontal assault and then take up the opposite challenge, which doubts even the narrow foundations for knowledge which we have so far been relying on.

A preliminary answer to blunt common sense is that it spoils the spirit of the chase. There is an ancient Greek story about a school of philosophers at Miletus, who were debating how many teeth a horse has. A young and green student, eager to help things along, dashed out and fetched a horse, so that they could count its teeth. For this he was very properly expelled. It is a good story, because it catches two points of view very prettily. From one, the philosophers are plainly being silly. How many teeth a horse has depends on the horse. Here fact trumps speculation. From the other, the student had missed the point of the exercise. The sages were seeking the why and wherefore of the matter and needed to arrive at a number which made sense in some ultimate scheme of things. Here the real, essential nature of The Horse is the crux and common–or–garden horses can wait. That no doubt sounds pretty silly too but it would not do so if we were discussing the place of theoretical order in modern physics. At some stage an ordered scheme would need to emerge so as to unify and explain a tangle of observations. When experiences refused to fit neatly into the scheme, the theory would not automatically be overthrown. There are ways of dealing with tiresome facts, along lines indicated before, and, in general, theory does not arise smoothly by the gradual refining of common sense.

All the same, it still seems perverse not to take solid, everyday physical objects for granted, when thinking about the furniture of Earth. For, whatever may be said about quarks in physics, a horse is a horse. The reply to this, however, is that no one is denying it. No one disputes that there are horses, in the sense that we succeed in talking to one another about the horses, which we plainly perceive. But this conversational success leaves it very much open just what we are doing and how we manage to do it. Common sense is welcome to insist on physical solids but it is – or should be – neutral about the relation between them, subjective experiences and mental judgements.

The view that we arrive at solid objects by having the mind digest experience with a power of its own is not, I grant, markedly common-sensical. But then neither is the view that solid objects are composed of electrical charges and discharges from the superinvisible components of unobservable particles. So there is going to be a puzzle somewhere about reality, theory and experience. The bee poses it before we arrive at solids and at least that makes it easier for laymen to think about. The reason for posing it there lies in the case for holding that knowledge needs foundations, however. If experience must be so construed that some reports of it have a truth guaranteed without proof or evidence, then it has to be private and subjective, with the public world secured precariously through the mind's active judgement. But what if the case for foundations is misconceived?

Cracks in the Foundations?

The case, as I put it before, is that not all our warranted beliefs can be justified by inferring them from others. There must be some whose truth is flatly given, to act as a foundation for the rest. Our knowledge of the world thus rests on reports of experience, which involve no possible risk of correction, since they would otherwise need to be justified further. Yet do we have and do we need such risk-free guarantees of truth? I shall invite you to look briefly at just one reason for disputing the need for foundations. Then I shall sketch an account of knowledge which does without them, and go on to point out some unsolved problems which it yields.

An effective challenge to the case for foundations would be to show that we cannot have them. Provided that the upshot is not merely to leave us with no way of knowing anything, the theory of knowledge will then need a fresh approach. Here is a challenge, which contends that communication involves a knowledge which cannot possibly rest on foundations. So far, in speaking of knowledge and of extending it by testing belief against experience, I have assumed that experiences can be described in words. This sounds a very harmless assumption, since they plainly can and, anyway, I have been describing them in words all along. But, harmless or not, it is certainly crucial. For, if your experiences are private to you and mine to me, we can share them only by conveying descriptions to each other. (That is not quite true, since you can hack me on the shin to show me what the pain is like or play me the music which moves you; but words do the bulk of the work.) We need to be able to share them because the judgements each of us makes about the furniture of Earth are judgements about what exists as much for other people as for oneself. Yet the foundations were sought in the manner of Descartes' *Meditations* by setting a single 'I' to winnow its own beliefs, until something wholly beyond doubt and correction remained. This something was so firmly subjective and private that it would not be shaken even by a strange discovery that other people were figments of the consciousness of this one central 'I'.

That being so, each of us must be able, in principle, to describe our own private experiences correctly and independently of how other people describe theirs. For instance, you have your own sensations of colour and can separate colours for yourself, even without knowing their public names. You could give each colour-sensation your own private name. Then learning the public name would be learning the rule which matches your private sensations to mine. What you used to call 'wolley' to yourself, you now call 'yellow'. Notice that this does not guarantee that you and I have the same experience. Indeed in one way we plainly do not, since yours remains peculiar to you and mine to me; but, more to the point, if you are systematically different from me, you will not find it out by learning to call daffodils 'yellow'. The public language succeeds only in calibrating the distinctions which each of us makes. It does not let us be sure that, if I could somehow experience the very sensation of yours which you call 'yellow', I would call it 'yellow' too. But I cannot climb into your head and, luckily, we can communicate without my having to.

The challenging objection is that this picture of language is nonsensical. People who already have a public language can use private names for experiences; but private names cannot be the building blocks of a public language. The objection can be made specific to talk about experiences or general for language at large. Specifically, think how we manage to talk about public objects like, say, beetles. To focus concentration, suppose that each of my two sons keeps a beetle in a box by his bed and refuses to let anyone else see inside. Even so, each can describe his beetle and they can compare notes. But that is because there are beetles (and other things) in the public world and because, in the final analysis, the boxes can be opened. Now suppose all beetles live in private boxes, each magically constructed so that only its owner can see inside. The boys can still describe their beetles but only in terms borrowed from talk about things which do not live in boxes. So suppose that all descriptive terms in our language are ultimately terms for things in magic boxes. Suppose, in other words, there was no going language to borrow from. Now neither boy can be sure what the other is saying about his beetle. Indeed it is unclear that both have beetles, since this implies that their pets are similar in ways which they cannot establish. That makes it unclear also whether either has a *beetle*. Conversely, since people do succeed in comparing notes, some uses of language to describe the world cannot depend on what is inside magically constructed, individually private boxes. Yet Descartes' whole strategy depends on being able to treat the mind as a private box.

This argument gains force if put as a special case of a broader one. Success in talking (even to oneself) depends on using words in the same sense on different occasions. 'Beetle', for instance, must mean the same when used by me now as by you and others before. Otherwise I do not mean what I seem to and perhaps mean nothing at all. What counts as 'the same' depends on rules, governing the right way to carry on and serving as the test of mistakes. These rules function typically as the rules of games do. The rules of a game not only police the game but also, so to speak, create it, in the sense that there are no chess pieces or moves before there are rules of chess. Even games for one, like Demon Patience with cards, have rules that answer a doubt, which I can raise even if I am playing patience, about whether I am playing correctly. In language games, as in card games, this doubt can be settled only by appeal to rules. Although I can invent a game called 'Inner Experience' with my own rules, I can decide whether I am keeping to my own intentions only by covert appeal to games like Public Description, which I did not invent. Otherwise whatever I do is as correct or incorrect as anything else. Hence, public rules of language and thought underlie private, individual ones; it cannot be the other way around. The moral is – or is often claimed to be – that Descartes' experiment, which shrank the world to himself and his private mental states, fails. It fails to show what lies at the bottom of our knowledge, because the language used to describe the bottom layer has no meaning left in it. Demon Patience, played under Descartes' private rules, cannot be the basic game.

I do not wish to endorse the moral here. There is fierce dispute about the merits of the argument and snap judgements are not to be made. I merely point it out as one way in which the classic case for foundations of knowledge has lately been attacked. Now let us see what happens to our ideas about knowledge and science without some unique starting point for the work of justifying beliefs by proof and evidence.

It might seem that there is no longer a problem about chairs and tables and the other solid objects of common sense. But there is still going to be a puzzle somewhere about experience, theory and reality. The novelty introduced by insisting on the mind's 'power of its own' was to make the mind active in gaining knowledge, instead of trying passively to record the world as it is. But even an active mind needs data of experience, reliable as material to work on and as an objective test for conjectures. Without foundations of knowledge, it seems, the active mind invades even the crucial moment of objective truth. We must be clear about the consequences, before deciding whether to welcome the invasion.

There are two classic sorts of limit to what a person can rationally believe. One is that beliefs must square with the known facts of the world. The other is that they must add up to a coherent system, free of contradiction. I have not said much about this latter limit but presumably it leaves more than one system of thought possible, even if arguments like the ones about space and time were to succeed in reducing the variety of them. Now, however, we are starting to suspect that 'the known facts of the world' have a surprising amount of play in them. What they are seems to depend on interpretation and on the rules of whatever public language a group of interpreters share. Foundations of knowledge would act as a sort of gold standard for claims to truth and it is alarming to go off the gold standard. Yet stable currencies are to be had without one and all may yet be well.

The threat is that without a foundation for known facts anything goes. Earlier we noticed that, when a conjecture failed the test of experience, it was not plain just which hypothesis was at fault. Refutation does not point the finger anywhere in particular. But it does not point nowhere at all. When our beliefs fail to square with the world, we have a choice of which to revise; but we cannot merely refuse to revise any of them. For instance flat-earthers must do something about the evidence that the Earth is round. A popular move is to conjecture that light travels in curves instead of straight lines. That explains why, for example, ships seem to drop away over a curved horizon, while truly remaining on the same flat surface. Ingenuity like this keeps the Flat-Earth Society going and, enjoyably, is properly scientific in spirit. Flat-earthers accept that they cannot have both the Earth flat and light travelling in straight lines; but they insist that the choice is theirs, not Nature's. Experience demands an adjustment somewhere and the demand is met provided the revised system is coherent *overall*.

That puts them in good intellectual company at present. The philosophical fashion is very much for scrapping the search for foundations and for making the mind active in spinning a coherent web of belief. Here is a glorious passage, in which the pragmatist philosopher W.v.O. Quine speaks of 'the myth of physical objects' as similar from the standpoint of the theory of knowledge ('epistemologically') to the myth of the Ancient Greek gods (from 'Two Dogmas of Empiricism' in *From a Logical Point of View*, 1961, the 1st and 4th paragraphs of section six):

> The totality of our so-called knowledge or beliefs, from the most casual matters of geography and history to the profoundest laws of atomic physics or even pure mathematics and logic, is a man-made fabric which impinges on experience only along the edges. Or to change the figure, total science is like a field of force whose boundary conditions are experience. A conflict with experience at the periphery occasions readjustments in the interior of the field . . . But the total field is so underdetermined by its boundary conditions, experience, that there is much latitude of choice as to what statements to reevaluate in the light of any single contrary experience. No particular experiences are linked with any particular statements in the interior of the field, except indirectly through considerations of equilibrium affecting the field as a whole . . .

As an empiricist I continue to think of the conceptual scheme of science as a tool, ultimately, for predicting future experience in the light of past experience. Physical objects are conceptually imported into the situation as convenient intermediaries – not by definition in terms of experience, but simply as irreducible posits comparable, epistemologically, to the gods of Homer. For my part I do, qua lay physicist, believe in physical objects and not in Homer's gods; and I consider it a scientific error to believe otherwise. But in point of epistemological footing the physical objects and the gods differ only in degree and not in kind. Both sorts of entities enter our conception only as cultural posits. The myth of physical objects is epistemologically superior to most in that it has proved more efficacious than other myths as a device for working a manageable structure into the flux of experience.

These striking images leave much to think about. Knowledge has become a man-made fabric, whose claim to truth (if that is still the right word) is its success in working a manageable structure into the flux of experience. Since neither the facts of experience nor the laws of physics, mathematics and logic are independent of us any longer, the mind is made active with a vengeance. That will seem a great improvement on treating it as a recording device. But just how much latitude of choice are we being given? At first glance, it seems almost total, with Homeric gods as one way of working structure into the flux and physical objects simply another. But slower reading shows that there are still constraints. A conflict with experience cannot be dealt with merely by dismissing the experience; so there is still some kind of external world. The adjustment cannot be made merely *ad hoc*, since there are prices to pay elsewhere for local adjustments and the result is governed by considerations of 'equilibrium'. Physical objects are superior to Homeric gods, because more 'efficacious'. In correcting the old idea of the mind as blank white paper (recall Locke on p.79), we are not being given an opposite *carte blanche*.

The 'middle way', then, does not abolish all constraints, even though the mind has become active in interpreting and has a choice about what to declare to be knowledge. That is just as well, since the danger of anarchy was coming close. But what shall we make of the constraints? One response is that they vindicate the old account of objectivity, which confronted the mind with some brute facts of an external world and bound it with some given laws of thought. In that case there is not much wrong with the argument for foundations after all and the puzzles set by making the mind active in its judgements remain acute for traditional reasons. I find this a congenial line myself. But the constraints might have a very different kind of source and I shall mention some suggestions, which do not take us back into the previous chapter.

Sources of Constraint

Instead of talking airily of the mind, we should perhaps be wondering about the brain. Could the final keys lie in the biology of the human brain or the way it stores and processes information? The short answer is that it is too early to say much. Biotechnology is in its infancy and the science of artificial intelligence has hardly begun to toddle. Notice, however, that the future progress of such studies is not just a matter of unearthing the facts. It is still very much an open question what sort of computer-style model is best for human abilities, which include interpreting, judging and the rest of our thinking. Nor is there anything short to say about the relation of mind to brain, except that it is a vexed topic, among the hardest and most argued over in the philosophy of mind.

Another suggestion is that there are social constraints on how we order experience and on what we believe or refuse to believe about the world. For instance, those Homeric gods were well suited to Homeric society. They served the function of all gods in lending significance to events in everyday life, in sanctifying its important episodes and in underwriting its moral imperatives. Also, since the Greek pantheon was not a smooth committee but more like a power struggle among lazy bandit chiefs, they explained turbulence and caprice in social life and in the workings of nature. In generalized form, the suggestion is that the intellectual world of a culture reflects social constraints, needs and tensions, which are the true source of intellectual limits to thought. That is the main direction of influence but, importantly too, intellectual order then serves to keep social life manageable. The idea is perhaps most familiar from the Marxist theory of ideology but one need not be a Marxist to favour some kind of 'sociology of knowledge'.

A crude version makes the members of a culture unduly stupid about the real character of their cherished beliefs. In a more refined one, people can see the connections between their intellectual and social worlds. That makes it more of an open question, however, which is the main direction of influence. For instance, science is rarely a self-contained activity and is often connected with the distribution of power in a society *via* religious belief and practice. When Kepler, the early seventeenth-century astronomer, described the task of science as 'thinking God's thoughts after Him', he was very conscious that the Church had institutional views on the science of the heavens. Descartes too was uneasy about charges of heresy – indeed his books only just escaped public burning on one occasion. On the other hand, a religious person of course expects to find God in the workings of nature and of course wishes to order social life with divine guidance. The sociology of knowledge works in both directions. The point is that it might help to explain why the science of one culture finds principles of nature self-evident which other cultures, with a different religion and social system, do not think even plausible. Constraints, which have a source in other realms of intellectual or social life, can seem like immovable foundations.

I am not pressing the case for even a refined sociology of knowledge without tracing connections in great detail. It would take more than a study of Ancient Greek beliefs about the gods of the sea to tempt one to look for political influences in the modern physics of subatomic particles. But the idea of social sources for intellectual constraints is instructive in another way. It spotlights an undeniable gap, where belief outstrips its warrants. The gap is a challenge to the stock notion of scientific progress as orderly advance to fuller knowledge. It is too quick to say that to be rational is merely to conform to socially convenient standards of rationality. But there is a real puzzle about what else is involved.

The puzzle has been posed starkly of late by Thomas Kuhn's book *The Structure of Scientific Revolutions* (1962). The schoolroom history of Western science is a tale of conjectures put to the test of experience and accepted or rejected accordingly. If accepted, they are gradually filled in with careful detail, until fit for reporting in official textbooks. That is how we came to know, for instance, that the Earth goes round the sun (not *vice versa*) along with eight other planets (not six). In Kuhn's history of science the story is very different. It is one of periodic revolutions in which the basic thought and theory suddenly get replaced for pretty shaky reasons. For example, Copernicus' new astronomy was rather inferior to the Ptolemaic system in its accuracy and predictions and remained so for at least another century. Kepler, who helped it along, put the sun at the centre of the solar system at least partly because it symbolized God the Father. In general, Kuhn argues, textbook science takes place within a 'paradigm', a set of broad assumptions, which are presupposed rather than tested and which govern the interpretation given to the results of experiments. So powerful are these 'paradigms' that, when they change, perception of the world changes with them. Since they are neither arrived at by proof and evidence nor properly refuted when they fall, there is a gross distortion in the pious schoolbook history of science.

Critics have complained that Kuhn has made too much of a difference between everyday science within a paradigm and revolutionary science when a paradigm collapses. If so, the true history is not as jerky as he suggests. But he is right about the role of broad assumptions, like Newton's laws of motion, in governing rather than awaiting the verdict of experience. At least, I hope he is, as the idea goes so well with the 'Wonder, Paradox and Vision' theme of this book! But this means, once again, that there are mysterious constraints on what comes to be accepted or rejected. They are mysterious in that the chapter on reasoning wholly fails to deal with them and the three since have merely made it plainer that they are there. The puzzle remains why, if they are not thrust on us by our biology or social situation, we are rational in choosing to rely on them.

The puzzle might go away, if it were just the familiar point that we cannot climb out of our heads, coupled with the question, Why not? But there seems to be too much choice involved. Take the parallel with ethics, where it looks plain that people make all sorts of moral judgements, without proper proof or evidence, and do so on the strength of ethical frameworks which differ markedly from place to place. Here, the point that moral judgements are human-centred and the lack of a universal, objective or absolute standpoint for comparing frameworks are often held to sabotage the pursuit of truth in ethics. This scepticism is commonly advanced by contrasting the human-centredness of ethics with the neutral objectivity of science. But it is turning out that all knowledge depends on judgements which are human-centred. The trouble with ethics seems to apply to all standards of reason.

The argument appeals by its use of the actual variety in paradigms, which is scarcely less obvious than the actual variety of moral frameworks. In neither case, however, does it follow that there is nothing fixed or universal. Complete frameworks may all differ and yet all have something in common. Indeed, some philosophers argue that, unless they did, it would not be possible to understand one from within the confines of another. For how can we grasp other people's ways of adjusting to experience, unless we can realize that we would find the response rational in their shoes? This move needs deep thought but it is arresting enough to block any quick conclusion from the fact that variety is rife.

That puts us back in Plato's cave, with fellow prisoners who belong to humanity at large, rather than to one particular culture. There do indeed appear to be some constraints on all thought, some assumptions about reason and experience, which we can neither avoid nor justify. The attempt to pin them down revives the traditional call for foundations of knowledge, even if the focus has to shift from the brute facts of sense-experience to the presuppositions of order in understanding the world. This said, the variety of frameworks is a useful reminder that many twentieth-century beliefs will one day seem parochial in their turn. It has to be admitted, however, that, if the traditional search had succeeded, I would have mentioned it.

Conclusion

I opened these three chapters with a promise to discuss the character of human knowledge in a way which set a problem for our belief that we have free will. I added, however, that paradoxes lay in wait.

The clearest threat to free will comes from a theory of knowledge designed for purposes of science. The roots of much recent philosophy lie in the seventeenth century, especially in Descartes' *Meditations* and the duel between the mind and the demon of scepticism. That also means roots in an account of nature as a realm of mass in motion governed by hidden forces and iron laws of cause and effect. There will not be ready scope for free action in a world where events must happen as they must. A theory of knowledge which ties our warrants for belief to the use of concepts designed for a seventeenth-century picture of nature will give trouble at its human end.

But that is all too specific. Science does not have to be Newtonian and the theory of knowledge need not be wedded to science. A less threatening account of science is most easily to be had by dispensing with iron laws of cause and effect. The Ant, for instance, operates with a notion of patterns in experience, which allow prediction from similar cases. That gives a softer and more flexible idea of cause and effect. In place of iron necessity in nature, we have patterns and probabilities. Causal laws become statistical regularities, which is all they need to be to make sense of the 'percolator' diagram of scientific method. This removes a palpable threat to human power to intervene in nature, although, as we shall find in chapter 9, it may leave a subtler one.

'Knowledge' thus needs defining so as not to imply a particular image of nature. Also, the definition should not rule out the pursuit of truth in, say, religion, ethics or literature. 'Justified, true belief' is a classic tag and one which sounds neutral enough. It also helps to make it clear what needs to be shown by any attempt at a two-world theory and why such theories are vulnerable to sceptics. This is not to say that the tag is accepted on all hands, and recent philosophy journals contain fierce disputes about it. But it will serve nicely for Invitation purposes.

The deeper threat to free will comes from the natural idea that knowledge is a passive affair of the mind registering a fact or truth. Maps and mirrors were the suggested images for the self-effacement which objectivity seems to demand. Certainly that has been the traditional idea, with the search for foundations ending in beliefs unsullied by imagination. If the knowing mind is a true mirror of an object, then we can know ourselves only as objects. It is perfectly possible to conceive of human beings as complex objects, we shall find, but the price is that free will is, at best, a mere conjecture.

The threat is apparently lifted by insisting that the mind is active, rather than passive, even in matters of perception. We were prompted by noticing that, when 'experience' was so construed that simple perceptions were guaranteed to be beyond doubt because their data were private and momentary, chairs, tables and elephants were banished to a second world beyond our ken. This account is especially contentious, in that it guarantees objectivity by making the data of perception wholly subjective. But other attempts to draw a strict line between what is objective and what is subject-centred also run into difficulties and, on reflection, it may seem a mistake even to try for self-effacement, since there needs to be scope for imagination in human knowledge. Rather, since imagination is no guarantee of truth, a better term is 'active judgement'. We know only after interpreting and judging – a process which relies on concepts and assumptions beyond proof and evidence. This makes the mind active in constructing our knowledge of the world and so makes it easier to maintain that we have free will.

But, as usual, quick solutions are not on offer. The mind cannot be so active that anything goes. There are still constraints on what we can rationally believe and the upshot is still an objective causal order to which we belong. If to possess free will is to be somehow internally self-causing or self-propelling, we have yet to square this idea with that of causal order; and, if not, I do not see how thinking in terms of a web of belief changes the problem. So I shall adjourn the topic to chapter 9. Meanwhile, whatever we want to say about the spinners, the image of knowledge as a web of belief still contains a paradox. It is that we cannot discover order in our experience without imposing it as we interpret; and, having imposed the order, we cannot know it to be independent of us.

Less grandly, it remains crucial that we cannot climb out of our own heads. By now, however, this is not a regrettable failure but a reminder that we are still at the meeting point of closed and open questions. The open ones are a bit unnerving, as Quine's remarks about the gods of Homer bring out. But, if physical objects like tables and elephants turn out to be cultural posits, it is wise to keep cool. Nothing in these chapters *proves* that reality consists of posits. Before deciding that there is paradox in reality, one needs to have finished adjusting one's set.

6

The Elusive 'I'

'I think, therefore I am,' Descartes reported after wrestling with the demon of doubt. The bedrock truth lay in the mind's 'I'. What exactly did he suppose this 'I' to be? It was a 'conscious thing', an individual entity, with a will and an understanding, directly aware of its own states and of itself. 'I' names something which is not my brain or body and is not governed by the laws of physical nature. There is one such something per person and each is cut off from others by the physical envelopes, which somehow house these immaterial selves. Each is known directly only to itself (and to God). Each is immortal.

He thus believed that he had dug down to what we call the soul in church and the self at home. It will seem pretty unlikely that an argument, which starts by asking how I know that I am not dreaming, can lead swiftly to an immortal soul; but that topic is not for now. This chapter is about the self of self-consciousness. It links with the last three by taking up the human element, which we finally stopped trying to eliminate from justified true belief and objective judgement. The opening question is what or who we humans are and how we know it. It will lead us to think of the self in relation to other people and hence, in chapter 7, to an enquiry about the basis of ethics and, in chapter 8, about our understanding of social life. That means a broader and looser theme for these three chapters than for the last trio, but their unifying aim is to construct enough of a portrait of human nature to give life to the promised discussion of free will in chapter 9.

Descartes is again a good starting point because so much of his account stays with us still. Most of us think of ourselves as individuals and mean something which Descartes would recognize. I, at least, have a strong sense of being a real, unique, self-conscious something, known to myself in a special way and better than to anyone else. I incline to believe that I am not (or not exactly) a physical thing and that my body, even my brain, is apparatus which *I* use. I am curious about the inner world of other people, because I have no direct contact with it (and not merely because I am puzzled to find myself cut off from it philosophically by the logic of the *Meditations*). Being a professional philosopher, I am aware that some of these other minds are fellow philosophers, who think that Descartes has marched us straight up a blind alley. But I find a great deal of truth in the self-portrait of the *Meditations* and there is a fair chance that you do too. In brief, Descartes' self is not 'all my I' and, even if it were, it would still be a good place to start.

Masks, Roles, Duties and Selves

As with Descartes' picture of nature as a machine, his view of the self was right for its historical context. Since it is easier to discuss the self, if one remembers that it is not a concept ready to hand in every culture, I shall here digress very briefly.

Historically it is hard to say just when the idea of a person as having or being an individual self arrived on the human scene. Think of those strangely carved and painted masks which hang on the walls of museums of ethnography, especially those from long ago. They are not merely decorative. Their strangeness lies in the elusive message they convey about who the wearer was. They assign him to a place among his kin or tribe and set him in relation to his gods and to his ancestors. The message is elusive not so much because we do not have the detail of these relationships, as because it embodies an understanding of self which we do not share. Somehow, the mask is personal because it identifies the wearer within a particular chronicle, which fuses memory with myth. It proclaims which ancestors the wearer *is* – or so anthropologists say and that surely makes deeper, if murkier, sense of what is baffling. In other words, there have been, and are, cultures where persons are thought of as expressions or extrusions of some corporate identity, celebrated in its own myth and extending over generations. I do not pretend to grasp this idea very well but I can see that it is not our own.

Our own culture has Ancient Greece among its roots. Here we find an easier idea of a person, but not ours. In Homer's story of the fall of Troy and the wanderings of Odysseus (or Ulysses) on his way home to Ithaca, the characters are always the bearers of social positions and roles. Their actions are performances in office and their fortunes are bound up with notions of duty in a world governed by capricious gods. Homer, it is plausibly said, has no word correctly translated as 'person' but only words for man as living human organism (the *Anthropos* of anthropology), for 'man' and 'woman' as social characters of a certain rank, for 'male' in contrast to 'female' and so on. The plays of Aeschylus and Sophocles from the fifth century BC are also concerned with conflicts of role and duty, with characters who make what they can of divine ordinance in disobliging circumstances. They are full of anguished inner conflicts, as with Sophocles' Antigone, who must decide whether to bury her slain brother, thus disobeying the king's command, or to leave him unburied, thus failing in her family duty. Yet, although inner and personal, such conflicts are socially structured and there seems to be no sense of pure self as distinct from social and physical ties. There is no hint in Sophocles of embodied souls trapped in a social fabric but in truth unique and separate.

The same reading can be given to what we know of early Roman history and law. But with Roman law there begins to emerge an idea of persons who possess rights just by not being barbarians; and presently Stoic moral teachings proclaim an idea of a brotherhood of man, which gradually extends to barbarians too. Even so, this is all a matter of rights and duties, now perhaps universal but not yet individual in the sense of being grounded in the uniqueness and peculiarity of each person. For that we must wait until Christianity comes to speak of the soul as 'a rational, indivisible, individual substance'. With the arrival of Protestant Christianity, in particular, it becomes fully possible to think of the soul as an immaterial being with a conscience directly responsible to God and not defined by its social and physical life. That is some centuries later and part of the general challenge to traditional ideas, which the Renaissance brings. The challenge is plainest in religious, social and political thinking and Descartes did not intend the *Meditations* as a contribution on these fronts. But his human-centred theory of knowledge belongs in this wider context and would not have carried conviction without it.

The point of this hasty excursion is that not every culture could be led to regard '*I* think, therefore *I* am' as an evident truth. In many it would not make sense and, for ours, it needs its history. At the same time, however, the history is less unambiguous than the last couple of pages made it sound. It is not a mere matter of fact when the idea of persons as individuals emerged. The grammar of every language has some kind of first-person singular, a grammatical 'I', which lets speakers pick themselves out uniquely. The moral system of every culture attributes some kind of personal responsibility even to persons conceived of in terms of clan membership or social roles. Although the concept of self has clearly evolved, it is debatable when it evolved from what. Conversely, Descartes' sharp distinction between inner self and physical body did not put a stop to the older idea of the soul as the animating principle of the body. That still flourishes in Christian creeds which insist on the resurrection of the body and in much current psychology and philosophical thinking. Descartes' '*Cogito*' is not a universal milestone on the road of progress but a specific and contestable claim about who or what each of us is.

It also matters that Descartes had set himself a specifically modern problem. The rapid advance of science seemed to show that nature is a fully programmed machine. Previous accounts had pictured the universe as shot through with purpose. Overall, there had been a divine master-plan, which was translated into scientific detail by discovering the purpose and proper function of each kind of creature. With this as the leading idea, there was no bewildering snag to seeing how human beings fitted in. They might be special in having free will but that meant only a special question about whether a person had performed an allotted function well or ill. Meanwhile, as there was no clear need for an ultimate distinction between the mental and the physical, persons could be thought of as animate, perhaps to a special degree but not in sharp distinction to other creatures. Admittedly, this is too smooth a reading and we have already noticed that puzzles about inner and outer worlds go back at least to Plato. But, under the Christian aegis, ethics and science were comfortable together in a framework of functions and purposes.

A fully programmed, mechanical, physical system can be purposive only in a remote way. It can be designed for a purpose and, to that extent, modern science does not conflict with the idea of a divine master-plan. But its everyday workings and detailed linkages are those of cause and effect. There is a very real snag in ascribing free will to a cog in a machine. Human bodies are physical, just as the bodies of mice, molluscs and melons are physical. There was a new urgency to old questions about what makes humans special. They had to be dramatically different from other creatures, or else some cherished beliefs about freedom would be lost. In this historical context, Descartes' distinction in kind between mind and body seemed to him the only move open to a convinced scientist who was also a convinced Catholic. The self was assigned firmly to the mental side of a frontier between different realms of being. As Sir Thomas Browne, author of *Religio Medici*, put it at the time,

> Thus is man that great and true Amphibium, whose nature is disposed to live, not only like other creatures in divers elements, but in divided and distinguished worlds.

'I think, therefore I am' is thus more than an answer to a question about what grounds our knowledge of things at large. It is also offered as a solution to a fresh problem of how to fit man into a world governed in all its physical detail by automatic laws of cause and effect. The clause which guarantees our privacy, by insisting that 'I' has mental states known only at second hand by anyone else, also guarantees our humanity. By now, however, it is no obvious platitude that 'I think, therefore I am.' Even if we were tempted to reply to the historical remarks about the lack of self in other periods and cultures that Descartes had put a modern advance in a nutshell, we cannot suppose him to have had any sort of final word.

The Ghost in the Machine

Three aspects of Descartes' 'I' are distinctive. One is the capture of our sense that each of us is enduring and unique by making each person an individual conscious substance. One is the division of the universe into mental and physical orders of being, with the self, as an agent blessed with free will, assigned to the mental. One is the grounding of knowledge in the special and private access which each has to a particular inner life and self. All three elements will be familiar, even if not quite in this way of describing them, since Descartes partly caught and partly shaped the everyday assumptions which most of us now readily make. But, as said, he did not thereby take an unquestionable step forward and the next task is to raise difficulties.

The picture is of the self as an 'angel in a machine', as a critic of Descartes put it. That catches the uneasy amalgam of spiritual being and mechanical body very well. A more secular and openly sceptical tag is used by Gilbert Ryle in *The Concept of Mind* (1948), where he calls Descartes' I 'the ghost in the machine', and makes it clear that he does not believe in ghosts. That book is a powerful attempt to show that the mind is not a thing but a set of abilities and dispositions. For instance, generosity is not a feeling, which causes me to give money to those in need, but the habit of giving. Self-knowledge is the knowledge which I have of my own character and dispositions; it does not differ in kind from the sort of knowledge which other people have about me or I about other people. Conversely, the body is not simply a machine, since we use terms for much of its activity which we do not apply to machines. There are, for example, no generous computers. To think of mind and body as Descartes did, says Ryle, is to make the error of peasants who see a steam locomotive for the first time and insist that there must be a spirit driving the pistons.

This attack sounds crude, if outlined in a few words, and should not be judged before reading *The Concept of Mind*. Without this peasant experience, it will seem that the replacement offered for mind and body is body alone (plus some ingenious abilities which our bodies have). But to say that there is no ghost in the machine is not to say that persons are machines. A similar point is to be made about another text to conjure with in this area, Wittgenstein's *Philosophical Investigations* (1953), with the famous argument about private languages, which I borrowed in the last chapter as an example of an attack on the idea that knowledge needs foundations. Descartes never doubts that he can describe the private experiences, which he would remain sure of, whatever a malignant demon was up to. Wittgenstein contends that any language rests on rules for making claims which can be publicly checked and gets its sense from there being things accessible to more than one person. We discover the human mind in talking about public human behaviour. Again, a crude sketch would make it sound as if only machines could be talked about and ghosts were nonsense. But Wittgenstein's text is more subtle and ambiguous. It too needs reading, before conclusions from the nature of language are pressed into service.

In these and other ways the suspicion has often been aired that the 'I' of 'I think, therefore I am' is an invention. Grounds of it are perhaps plainest, when it comes to the problem of Other Minds. The question is, How can one person know what goes on in the inner life of another? If each person is an 'I', a ghost in a machine, with an inner life of private events and objects, the problem is notably awkward. The apparent answer is that I know how I act, when in a given private state, and so, if I see you acting in like manner, I can infer that you are in like state. For instance, I know what feeling produces my gasp of pain when I sit on a spike; so, when you spike yourself and gasp, I know that you feel the same. Provided that such basic analogies work, we can build up a complex language which allows talk of more nuanced feelings and the rest of inward life to be understood by both of us.

But, for reasons by now familiar, the inference is very shaky. It goes neither by proof nor by evidence. It can hardly be a matter of logic that what acts as if in pain is truly in pain, since logic does not rule it out that you are only a cunningly programmed robot, a machine with no ghost. Since there is proof (in the sense used in this book) only where the premises (my knowledge of myself, my behaviour and your behaviour) could not be true, and the conclusion (statements about your inner being) false, I have no proof of your inner being. Evidence, on the other hand, works by reasoning that what has been found in similar cases holds for the next case also. But there are simply no known cases. No one has ever made a direct comparison between the inner and outer states of two different people; no one is directly aware of more than one self or ghost in more than one machine. So there is no evidence for other minds either. Hence the argument from analogy is hopeless from the start.

That may seem too drastic an objection. When you infer that I am in pain by analogy with what you would be feeling, if you were gasping as I am, that is one analogy which I can check, since I know whether I am in pain. Does that not give me the needed entry? The answer, I fear, is 'No'. I must first be justified in believing that the basis of your inference is your comparison of your inner and outer states; and that is precisely the move which is blocked, until I have solved the Other Minds problem. In an account of knowledge which rests squarely on 'I think, therefore I am', *all* knowledge about other ghosts in other machines is secondary; and none can be presupposed in showing that I sometimes have it.

The same snag does for the thought that there is a problem of Other Minds only because telepathy is rare. There are well-evidenced cases of people who are close in spirit sharing a mental experience over great distances. Even a single case of one 'I' directly aware of the inner world of another would show that access is possible; even a few would make the analogy respectable. The snag surfaces when we ask how many mental experiences are involved in a case of telepathy. If the communication is ghost-to-ghost, the answer must be two separate experiences, one belonging to each ghost. That simply restates the puzzle of how we know these separate experiences to be near enough identical. Telepathic ghosts would get along splendidly but they would not have a built-in solution to the Other Minds problem.

That drives us to try finding a solution in the very fact of everyday communication. How could we talk to each other about our experiences, unless we each had experiences to talk about? Unluckily, however, sentences can in general make sense without what they state or imply being true. Ancient Greeks conversed successfully about the activities of the gods and, in doing so, presupposed the existence of these invisible beings. But their words made sense, whether or not there were gods to speak of. On the other hand, Ancient Greek talk of gods, while not proving the existence of gods, may prove the existence of Ancient Greeks! Communication involves shared beliefs; and shared beliefs need minds to share them.

Yet computers communicate. The quick retort is that they do not mean what they seem to say. But that is to restate the problem again. Might it not be that I mean what I say but you are a cleverly programmed robot? The tempting reply is that I can mean what I say only if you mean what you say; but no reason has been given so far. According to Ryle, Wittgenstein and others, no reason can be given, while the puzzle remains one of putting ghosts in touch with ghosts. The problem solves, they maintain, only within a frame of reference, where self-knowledge is learnt by way of knowledge about other people; and that exactly reverses Descartes' order of inferences. I am not endorsing this line, merely showing how it comes in, but it is to be taken seriously.

None of this will have shaken your conviction that the best authority on your inner states of mind is you. Yet that too can be challenged. Freudian psychology, for example, insists that self-knowledge is often hard to come by, precarious and only to be had by learning to see oneself with detachment. Inner life, say Freudians, is much shaped by an unconscious, which is not open to direct inspection. Other psychologies of the mind work with other sorts of symbols but share the belief that individuals do not always grasp the symbols which influence their inner states. For behavioural psychologies there is no basic reason at all to think individuals best placed to understand themselves; and, in general, there is the vexed question of whether mental life is truly governed by the workings of the brain, about which little is known, especially to you and me.

But I do not think that claims to self-knowledge should yield to these kinds of frontal assault. 'I think, therefore I am' does not imply that I cannot ever be wrong about my inner world. There is room for self-deception, confusion and incomplete self-awareness, provided that there is some self-knowledge which needs no proof or evidence. Since psychologists have to interpret their own observations, they too are caught up in the earlier discussion of the mind's role in judgement. Whatever that established applies to psychology too. If Descartes survived those earlier arguments, his concept of a person does not fall to the findings of modern psychology.

Something like it is certainly needed by anyone who construes raw experience as private, mental events. In that case, our beliefs about the solid, durable things in the world are in a flimsy relation to the experiences which are evidence for them. What makes an experience now and an experience a moment ago experiences of the same elephant has something to do with their being experiences belonging to the same person. The Way of Ideas needs a self to unify the ideas. This point loses its particular force, if we stop thinking of experience as private, mental events; and this book has not reviewed other kinds of account. But there will still be the case for insisting that knowledge involves active interpretation and, with it, for thinking of persons as interpreters. 'I interpret, therefore I am' will remain a very defensible move.

This is not to uphold Descartes in full. It is only to deny that he is vulnerable to science in his claim that the basic knowledge is self-knowledge, including knowledge that the self is a conscious thing. Equally, it is a fair retort to those who try dissolving the mind into a bundle of dispositions and abilities, or find it visible in the public uses of language, that abilities need to be a person's abilities, and words a person's words. To that extent, the understanding of behaviour points inward. But it is not plain that it points to an 'I', if that means a ghost in a machine. The problems of Other Minds is only one example of the snags of ghost-hunting and it is enough to disturb a simple trust in persons as spiritual blobs. The self was presented as the thing best known to us but is so far proving oddly elusive.

Self in Action

Sir Thomas Browne called man 'that great and true Amphibium'. Perhaps the trouble lies here, with the sharp line drawn between mind and body. Do we really dwell in 'divided and distinguished worlds'?

In some ways we do. All along it has been very natural to talk of mental events and physical events, without assuming even that each event of one sort goes with an event of the other. The language for speaking of the mind is one of perceptions, feelings, beliefs and desires. For the body or brain it is one of muscles, bones, neurons and synapses. We often use one without regard for what, if anything, we could say in the other. 'Divided and distinguished worlds' sounds a possible summary, at least if we know how the worlds connect. Well, do we not? While you are reading this book, your brain fills with data, your mind makes sense of them and, when you turn the page, your mind gives the order and your brain carries it out. No event in the sequence is both mental and physical, yet messages pass with success.

I shall have to leave it to you to decide whether in general it is truly possible to tell two stories about two sequences in two languages and then connect the stories in a coherent way. It is not plainly impossible and the question is a complex one in the philosophy of mind. My guess is that you will find a need for a concept which bridges the gap between thought and behaviour. At any rate it is interesting to explore the effect of introducing one and that is what I propose to do. The concept is action. Even if the action of turning a page might seem to fall readily into mental cause and physical effect, not all actions do. Let us take one which does not.

To lead in, here is a snatch of dialogue between Holmes and Watson from 'Abbey Grange' in Conan Doyle's *The Return of Sherlock Holmes*. Watson is, as usual, perplexed:

> 'Is there any point to which you would wish to draw my attention?'
> 'To the curious incident of the dog in the night-time.'
> 'The dog did nothing in the night-time.'
> 'That was the curious incident,' remarked Sherlock Holmes.

(It was curious and crucial because it proved an alleged intruder to have been well known to the dog, which was trained to bark at intruders.) The dog did nothing and meant nothing by it, although that in itself gave Holmes the clue. Contrast the case of the dog with those where people do nothing on purpose. A witness can influence a trial by leaving bits of evidence out. A spy can send a message, by not putting a small ad in *The Times*. A chess player can set a trap by not moving an unguarded knight. Doing nothing on purpose is doing something.

This suggests that there is not always a division into mental causes and physical effects. The chess player moves, say, a bishop and that is a physical effect. But there are dozens of moves thereby not made and just one of them constitutes the setting of the trap. To understand what has happened, then, we need to pick out the fact that the unguarded knight has not been moved. We must read into the physical event a meaning which it genuinely has but which does not belong to the physical description. The story does not divide into the player's intention (mental) and the trap set (physical); but it is a reading of the world in a language of action.

The same seems to me true of actions, like turning a page, where there appears to be a break between intention and effect. To explain what happens we need to describe the paper rectangle as a page, thus giving it, so to speak, a human dimension. We are telling a human story in which the events are what persons do. There is also a physical story, in which things move about but no actions occur, and a mental story in which plans are laid but no actions occur either. I do not myself think that the action story is a simple sum of the other two. It is a story of persons and I doubt that it breaks down into one about minds and one about bodies.

In that case, the self is seen in the action story, although elusive in the other two. 'Seen' is partly the right word and partly not. In the language of action, I see a person turn a page, whereas in the other languages I can be said to see only a page being turned by fingers or else nothing at all. Yet there is, presumably, more to persons than the actions which they perform. Your actions are done by *you* and this little word makes a further claim. To bring the point out, take a step back down the historical trail which leads to the self and think of persons as social actors on the stage of social life.

When we watch a marriage ceremony, we see the bride and groom plight their troth under the eye of the priest. That is a summary of the action in the language of action and it mentions 'bride', 'groom' and 'priest'. Yet we do not suppose that these actors are fully described by these labels. Bride and groom are playing their parts only for the time being and even the priest, whose office is more permanent, has more to him. Even granted that bride and groom have other, more lasting roles too and that the priest's role has many facets, we think of them as more than the sum of their social performances. That, we believe, is why old notions of 'self' failed to capture what is at the core of being a person, the man or woman behind the mask.

If this distinction applies here, it applies also to everyday actions. In the witness box we see witnesses; at the chess board we see chess players. From this angle a language of action does not give us a direct view of persons. What it does is to import into the perspective a system of rules, conventions, signs and symbols, without which action would lack intention and motive. But, if there is more to being a person than performing by the rules which give meaning to action, then it is still eluding us.

Whether there is more to it is a vexed question. The social system of roles and meanings is not rigid or explicit. It does not usually dictate who shall marry whom or what precise move the chess player plays next. It leaves room for personal choice and responsibility. Furthermore, it has to be learnt and this process is, often at least, one of self-discovery or even of self-creation. There are limits, with some actions being required and others forbidden but, within the limits, people can plausibly be said to give shape to their own lives. The chapter started with an historical sketch, suggesting that the self did not emerge until Christianity hit on the individual soul. If this is taken to imply that there is no self-direction earlier, it is misleading. When Ancient Greeks said 'I', they did not mean what Descartes does but they were ascribing personal aims and responsibility to their actions. There is a powerful case for holding that self-knowledge is gained through social action, since persons (unlike babies) are born in the establishing of a consistent style for very varied occasions.

That paragraph would make more sense to a social theorist than to a trained philosopher. In line for once with common sense, most professional philosophers insist that, in thinking of oneself as being the same person from year to year, one cannot be referring just to roles, social responsibilities and particular styles. Reference has to be to the *person* who performs, is accountable and brings individual character to the exercise. This counter-case is powerful too and, being mounted in the tones of pure reason, tends to sound less culture-bound than the other. As to that, however, even the pursuit of pure truth has to be in an historical context and ours is shot through with individualism. The case may well be right but it should not be allowed the unfair advantage of assuming what it seeks to prove.

Conclusion

How is the 'I' of 'I think, therefore I am' faring by now? Various doubts about it have been aired. The clearest is that, if each of us is a mental ghost in a physical machine, none of us can have proof or evidence that there are any others. It is hard enough, as we saw in earlier chapters, to infer from the inner self and its experiences to the outer world. The further inference to other inner worlds seems pure speculation. This may not be conclusive but it is certainly a motive for trying to replace the ghost with something more robust.

On the other hand, it is not so easy to exorcise it altogether. The belief that persons are not just machines is stubborn. One reason, crucial for the Way of Ideas and presumably of wider scope too, is that, if experience is construed as private, it needs a self to hold it together and to organize it as evidence of a physical world. But, as this would be the wrong way to construe experience, if we were just machines, the stubbornness may be misplaced. However, some famous arguments from the primacy of public behaviour or public language do not reduce persons to machines. They are better taken as directed against the separation of mind and body, by which man becomes a 'great and true Amphibium'. The point of attack is that actions cannot be broken up into a psychological component and physical component. Even if they could, there is also a puzzle about the crossing of the frontier from one to the other, since no inseparable hybrid events, however tiny, are allowed.

That suggests 'action' as a unifying concept with fresh implications. Perhaps actions are what *persons* do and that is why persons vanish, if one considers only a mental story or only a physical one. The self is to be found in action, with self-knowledge being what actors learn from their special perspectives on their own performances. The point about the public character of language might then come in as one about the social character of self-shaping performances, with the result that the self is best seen in social action on the social stage. Yet that sounds more of a throwback to older ideas of the self than will appeal to modern individualists and the hunt continues.

That leaves several lines to pursue into the Philosophy of Mind and its connections with theories of knowledge and of language. Without following them, I cannot be more definite about the concept of a person. But it is clear that there is something special about persons and hence about our understanding of persons. A ready thought is that it arises because our actions have moral significance and we have moral responsibility for them. Certainly the portrait of human nature, which gives trouble with the problem of free will, is a moral portrait. The next chapter sets about drawing it.

7

The Ring of Gyges

Modern science has robbed the natural world of moral purpose. The fall of the sparrow occurs because of the failure of its cardio-vascular system, not because the gods have decreed that its time is up. Formally the one explanation does not exclude the other, since the gods may still have decreed the chain of events which kills the sparrow. There is room both for a science of animal life and for a religion which makes heaven the final reason for what happens on Earth. But even a compromise is a defeat for the older view that every event has a meaning or moral purpose, which is directly part of its explanation. The 'how?' of science has largely taken over from the 'why?' of religion and meanings have retreated from the picture of nature to its frame. Formally that is a compromise but in practice 'how?' tends to matter more than 'why?'.

A world without meaning in nature is a threat to ethics. Questions of right and wrong are no longer all of a piece with other questions about what is so. Scientific enquiry into abortion, for instance, reveals its medical and social effects and the various attitudes to the practice among groups of people. But it stops firmly short of settling whether abortion is morally wrong. Even if every society and every person were of one mind, it could still be asked whether they were mistaken; and science would have no further help to offer. At any rate, this is a frequent modern claim about the relation of facts and values and it is easy to see how it has arisen.

The threat to ethics disturbs some views of human nature and suits others. It disturbs, for instance, those that try to find an objective meaning of life in human experience or that rely on there being absolute standards of right and wrong in the fabric of the universe. It suits, for instance, those that portray human beings as no more than complex machines or complex animals and have no patience with high-falutin talk of absolutes. Keeping to my general theme, however, I shall address myself to readers with mixed reactions. On the one hand, it is immensely liberating to escape from absolute moral precepts which glumly sanctify the disapproving authority of persons in power. On the other hand, it is unnerving to face the thought that all ethics are arbitrary, including one's own. A mixed reaction goes nicely with the individualist sort of picture of ourselves that has been taking uneasy shape in previous chapters. As with knowledge and self-knowledge, we shall be caught between the private and the public. This time the tension will be between private and public interests, with a central puzzle about prudence and morality. The puzzle is yet another which goes back to Plato – hence the mysterious title of the chapter.

Before we go any further, I should give warning that I shall be giving ethics a slant which favours some recent ways of thinking about the subject and by-passes others. The chapter's opening mention of modern science leads readily to a doubt whether values can be objective and whether we can have knowledge in ethics. In earlier times, science had sought to know the cause, function, purpose, reason, value and meaning of things in a single, integrated enquiry. Modern science, by contrast, has come to distinguish sharply between cause and meaning, helped by ideas of scientific method which identify causes while excluding values and meanings altogether. (To be precise, people's values and various sorts of meanings are objects of study for the social sciences but not in hope of arriving at the meaning of life. Some sciences still recognize functions, purposes and reasons; but in a similar spirit of neutrality about their higher significance.) This creates a central modern problem for ethics, when we ask how moral beliefs can be rational or how moral statements can be known to be true. The two leading modern answers are introduced below in the sections headed 'Moral reasons' and 'The pursuit of happiness'.

This is certainly a common way to discuss ethics and enough to keep us busy. But I do not mean to imply that it is the only way. For instance, one can start by thinking about good and bad emotions or about notions of authenticity and moral identity. Then other roads open up, for example into virtue-ethics or existentialism; and a similar point needs making about alternatives to the approach taken to social philosophy in the next chapter. With this large caveat, however, the roads which we shall be exploring are major ones.

Let us start with a general reason for wondering about ethics. There is no mistaking the wide variety of moral beliefs. (Try to think of one sexual taboo, apart perhaps from incest, which everyone accepts. Or notice how many moral attitudes are connected with the rules of property and consider how very diverse property arrangements are.) The point needs no labouring but is not crucial in itself. Scientific beliefs, after all, vary greatly too, especially when scientific institutions are not pervasive and powerful. The reason for wonder comes when we call for rules of proof or evidence for moral conclusions. Indeed it springs up even earlier, when we look for a single moral fact which we know from experience.

David Hume made the point famously in his *Treatise of Human Nature* (Book III, Part I):

> Take any action allowed to be vicious; wilful murder, for instance. Examine it in all lights, and see if you can find the matter of fact or real existence, which you call *vice*. In which ever way you take it, you will find only certain passions, motives, volitions and thoughts.

In other words, you might expect to find some fact about an obviously vicious murder which makes it vicious. But the only facts are those like blood on the corpse, hate in the killer's mind, pity or anger among the bystanders and other information, of it seems, a morally neutral kind. Even if you do not suppose that right and wrong are a matter of eyesight or the other four senses, you may think that there is a sixth, moral sense. Hume is sure that there is not, unless it is merely the way we know our own sentiments of approval and disapproval.

This might not matter, if moral facts could be reached by proof or evidence. But Hume goes on to show that neither route is open. To paraphrase him, a proof that wilful murder is vicious would need a true statement from which to work deductively. If this premise were a moral statement (for instance that life is sacred), then the question would simply become how we know that it is true. (How shall we prove that life is sacred?) If the premise were factual (for instance, that murder horrifies people), then the conclusion would not follow from it in logic. On the other hand 'Evidence' is even less promising. It is hopeless to argue that wilful murder is vicious because it is like other vicious acts, when the snag is precisely that there are no established cases to work with. There is no appealing to evidence, until after Hume's challenge has been answered.

This line of argument retains a huge influence. It encourages slogans like 'facts never imply values' or 'you cannot get from "is" to "ought"' or 'ethics is just value-judgements', which have great impact. Although it relies on more of an Ant's theory of knowledge than we were willing to accept earlier, it disturbs the parallel between truth in ethics and truth in science. If you learnt at your parent's knee that 'murder is wrong' is a fact as firm as any known to science, the lack of parallel is a shock.

It is easy to take flight at this point and abandon the belief that we know right from wrong. There are two fashionable and comforting ways of doing so, which it will be useful to have out in the open before taking up the question of moral knowledge in earnest. One makes morality a matter of social norms and the other a matter of private conscience.

The study of murder in fact finds more than 'passions, motives, volitions and thoughts'. It also finds a fabric of laws and social customs governing who can or cannot be killed with propriety. Variations are large. For instance it is (or has been) a duty in some places to avenge the murder of a kinsman or to kill a deformed child or to stone an adulteress to death or to exterminate members of a rival

clan or to burn heretics. In different places some or all of these habits
are forbidden but others, like human sacrifice, infanticide or hanging
for theft, are smiled upon. The tempting conclusion is that objective
morality is a fiction, which each society dresses up in its own way and
passes off as fact, perhaps for reasons of state. There is no need to
make a conspiracy of it, because the fiction is so compelling that
those who administer it often believe it themselves. But it is a fiction
none the less and there is nothing more ultimate than local law and
local custom.

The conclusion can be resisted. In the first place, the variety may
be only superficial. Some of it, at least, may arise because the same
precept is applied differently in different settings. For instance, it may
be that Britons and Eskimos share a norm of concern for their old
folk, which leads the Eskimos, given their bleak existence and their
beliefs about life in the next world, to leave their old people on ice-
floes to die, and leads the British to put theirs in old people's homes.
Underlying this (rather implausible) thought is the serious suggestion that all societies need a public morality as social glue and hence
that the variety must somehow involve similar solutions to equivalent problems. I would need much persuading that diversity vanishes, when careful comparisons are made, but it is worth thinking
about. In the second place, variety does not mean that everyone is
right. Different societies have also held very different beliefs about
the solar system; yet that does not make astronomy a fiction. I shall
not press this point, as it seems to beg the question of whether ethics
compares with science. But, formally speaking, variety is no proof
of anything.

The comforting move is to infer that each set of norms is binding
in its own place and time: 'In Rome do as the Romans do', in the
sense that one *ought* to obey Roman laws in Rome. This drops the
idea of absolute moral precepts but without making morality
arbitrary. The snag, however, is that local norms genuinely bind,
only if it is *objectively* true that one should obey local ordinances. That
restores just the sort of claim to objectivity which this line has just
abandoned.

Those taking the other line of flight are quick to agree. Their guiding thought is that moral precepts are *subjective* standards, which individuals set for themselves. It is a fiction to rope in God or nature as sources of moral authority, and 'society' is, for these purposes, fiction too. In Rome one has no moral duty whatever to do as the Romans do. Moral duties exist, if at all, only in the sense that individuals create their own. If I choose to adopt the standards of my (or any other) society, they become my own; but I cannot be criticized for refusing.

There is a sly ambiguity here. Does 'my own' mean 'adopted by me' or 'true for me'? It is a liberating idea that my morals are up to me, yours up to you, and no one is entitled to impose. But this does not make conscience a source of genuine obligation. If my 'conscience' is merely my own voice, appeal to it cannot justify my belief that I should obey it. Still less can it justify the general statement that everyone should obey conscience. Those claims require an objectivity to the voice of conscience, even if one so ordained that each voice (when authentic) binds only one person. Nor does the liberating idea imply tolerance. If I turn racist, I make intolerance 'my own' and may well be utterly sincere in my hatreds. There is no counter to racism, unless we distinguish firmly between 'adopted by me' and 'true for me' and insist that I cannot justify a moral view even for myself simply by adopting it. We should also be clear that the traditional claims of, for instance, Protestants that the dictates of one's conscience are morally binding presuppose an objective scheme of things, with conscience in direct contact with God. (Besides, Protestants have always held that only an 'examined' conscience truly binds.) Similarly, traditional liberalism, while preaching tolerance, does not tolerate all views indiscriminately. It does not tolerate views which involve harm to others against their will. In short, tolerance and subjectivity do not go together.

Morality, Self-interest and Duty

All the same, both lines of flight set a question over objectivity. This is a good moment to make it a general, sceptical one with Hume's challenge broadened so as to call all kinds of moral belief into doubt. Think of morality as a set of reasons for doing what, otherwise, you might have no reason to do. Suppose, for instance, that the prize which you covet can be yours only by cheating or that the pleasures which you fancy are to be had only by violence. Then there is a tension, often described as one between self-interest and morality. Without stopping to decide whether this is the right description for the moment, let me assume that we all feel a pull between 'I want to' and 'I shouldn't' or, to put it the other way, between 'I should' and 'I do not want to'. The moral reason is supposed to be always strong and, in good people, decisive. What gives it its strength? Why, indeed, are so-called moral reasons for action any reason at all?

Plato sets the problem memorably in Book II of *The Republic* by means of a fable. Once upon a time in Lydia, a shepherd called Gyges was minding his flock, when a chasm opened in the ground. Being adventurous, he climbed down into it and found astonishing things, among them a bronze horse, which was hollow and fitted with doors. He peeped through and saw a corpse of more than human size, with a gold ring on its finger. He took the ring and climbed back out. Later, at a shepherds' meeting, he was twiddling the ring on his finger and turned the bezel inwards. Everyone started to act as if he was no longer there. He had become invisible, until he turned the bezel back. Armed with this advantage, he presently got himself included in a deputation to the king of Lydia. On arrival at the palace he seduced the queen, murdered the king with her help and seized the throne. He then reigned for many years in great glory.

The job of the fable is to set aside any reason for virtue stemming from self-interest. The ring means that Gyges can get away with what he likes. He can do what morality forbids and do it without penalty. Indeed, if he is clever about it, he can also collect all the public rewards of virtue, which people give to those they trust and applaud. The question is whether he still has any reason to abide by the moral rules. If not, then morality turns out to be only an external device for stopping people getting their own way. The self-interested person, who can get away with it, fares better 'at the hands of both gods and men'.

This is not Plato's own conclusion. It is a challenge which he puts into the mouth of one of his characters for Socrates to wrestle with. Is there reason to be moral, even when it does not pay? The question is fairly independent of quite what one means by 'being moral' and 'paying'. To pose it we need presume only that there is a systematic difference in how we would behave with and without taking morality into account. There are moral reasons for doing x and other reasons for doing y: when and why precisely are the moral reasons stronger?

It is no answer, then, that in a society, where roles are strongly defined and people's lives woven deep into the social fabric, Gyges' temptations would not occur. He might then have different forbidden aims; but the tension would still be there. Besides, we nowadays find nothing odd in the story, as it stands. Although the fable is about barbarous Lydia and not civilized Athens, Plato is plainly able to think of the self as something personal, whatever history may have suggested to the contrary at the start of chapter 6. Our own fancy may not be for queens and thrones but we understand the promptings of private self-interest very well. Egoists seem in a strong intellectual position in taking what they want, provided that they can get away with it. They will injure other people, of course. But what can make it *rational* for them to care about that? It may be that some of them happen to care about their victims – perhaps Gyges loved his royal wife – and, if so, have less reason to injure them. But this alters where their self-interest lies, rather than introducing a reason to act against it.

Self-interest, then, is not to be confused with mere selfishness. Martyrs are not (usually) selfish, in the sense of seeking to benefit only themselves, but may still be self-interested, in the sense of giving their own interests priority over other people's. The difference is not wholly clear, however, without querying the relation of interests to desires. We often talk as if those who go after what they want are serving their own interests. But think of gold-loving King Midas, in another Ancient Greek story, who was granted one wish by the gods and rashly wished that whatever he touched would turn to gold. He was soon sorry, especially when he kissed his daughter and she turned to gold too. He had got just what he wanted, but it was not in his interests to have it.

That complicates the fable of Gyges. We need to be sure that his dishonesty truly paid. He is like a man who cheats his way to a prize. Few prize-winners want the trophy itself, even if it is made of solid gold. They want the achievement, the respect of their rivals, the glory and applause. These things are not to be had by cheating. The loser respects a winner who truly beat him. The crowd's applause is for the best athlete. The cheat gains the outward symbols but they are hollow, because they do not signify what they seem, even though everyone else believes that they do. Gyges ended up rich in false currency, having debased the measures of his success. The result beat being a shepherd, I dare say, but it lacked a dimension. If his self-interest lay there, then only honesty truly pays. When it is asked whether it pays to *be* honest or merely to *seem* honest, the unthinking reply is that if one can get away with it, seeming achieves the same and is much less costly. On reflection, however, seeming does not produce the same result.

This shows only that self-interest is not to be equated with hasty desire. Whether it coincides with well-considered desire, whose achievement would truly give lasting satisfaction, must wait for later. Assume for the moment that it does, so that Gyges can still be given different advice by self-interest and by morality. Assume that he and the queen lived happily ever after. Did he act rationally in making use of the ring? A natural reply is, 'Yes, but not morally'. That the reply is natural shows how readily we contrast 'rational' and 'moral'. To see what it comes to, however, we must next explore the idea of morality.

Moral Reasons

It sounds odd to ask whether morality pays. It suggests that one needs a further reason for doing what 'morality' advises one to do. The more usual idea is that the moral course should be followed for its own sake and not because gains outweigh losses. Moral reasons, then, do not so much outweigh other reasons as trump them. The difference is clearest in the familiar contrast between duty and pleasure. The stern voice of duty bids us put pleasure aside, do our duty and damn the consequences. The soldier who disobeys orders may only plead a higher duty as a reason for refusal. Trumps must be met with higher trumps. What exactly constitutes this special quality of moral reasons?

A classic answer was given by Kant in *The Foundations of the Metaphysic of Morals* (1785). Moral reasons are, as he put it, universal and categorical. To mend a fuse, you ought to switch off at the mains; to be polite, you ought to say 'Please' and 'Thank you'. These 'oughts' are not moral 'oughts', however. They apply only if you want to mend the fuse safely or want to be polite; and you have a choice about that. Sometimes you may have other, stronger reasons for taking risks or being rude. By contrast, you ought to keep your promises, whether you want to or not. That is a moral imperative which applies categorically and regardless of all but higher moral imperatives. It also applies universally, in a way which rules out special pleading. You cannot maintain that everyone should keep his promises except you. Nor can you be right in your treatment of me, unless I would be equally right to treat you in the same way, were our positions reversed. 'Universal' echoes the New Testament command 'to do unto others as you would that they should do unto you'; or, in the terser words of the proverb, 'to do as you would be done by'.

Kant's own wording of the supreme command of duty was, 'Act as though the maxim of your action were by your will to become a law of nature.' An important corollary was 'to treat every rational being, whether in yourself or in another, never as a means only but always also as an end.' The broad idea is easy to see and accept but it is less clear quite what it implies. For instance, the 'maxims' referred to presumably need not be completely general. When the Gestapo ask the whereabouts of your Jewish friends, you could presumably will the maxim 'tell the truth, except to evil men', rather than 'tell the truth always'. ('No parking, except on Saturdays' is as 'universal' as 'No parking'.) So it is no longer clear what exactly counts as special pleading or how to avoid immoral maxims like 'respect the religions of all except Hindus'. None the less, you will probably agree that Kant has captured a basic form of a moral reason and share his hope that, by deriving principles of duty 'from the universal concept of a rational being', one can sort out any awkwardness.

Gyges, by these tests, has used the king, queen and others as means, rather than as ends, and in ways which he would not care for, were positions reversed. If everyone behaved like him, the social fabric would collapse; he clearly would not want his example to become a law of nature. (Criminals have every reason to believe in law and order: they need to be able to count on law-abiding behaviour by everyone else!) But the puzzle remains why it would have been rational to follow moral reasons rather than those of self-interest. Before trying to say, I want to sketch a different approach to ethics.

The Pursuit of Happiness

'The first proposition of morality is that to have moral worth an action must be done from duty,' Kant declared. Not everyone would agree. One can argue that other motives count for as much or more – love, for instance. One can also argue that motives matter less than consequence, with moral worth judged not by whether people mean well but by whether they do good. Formally speaking, these alternatives are not in direct collision with an ethic of duty, since there could be, for example, a duty to love thy neighbour or to produce the best consequences. But the contrasts are often made.

The most robust ethic of consequences is Utilitarianism or the theory which defines the moral worth of actions by the net amount of happiness they produce. A familiar version bids us think in terms of 'the greatest happiness of the greatest number'. How sharp-edged the formula is depends on how 'happiness' is defined, with candidates ranging from 'pleasure' to 'tranquillity of soul', and it is worth wondering what kind of happiness Gyges gained. But the crucial point about every version is that each person counts for one and, hence, that Gyges' happiness is not to be bought at the expense of other people's. As with duty, there is to be no special pleading or bias to oneself. Unlike an ethic of duty, however, utilitarianism is willing to trade off one person against others and that can make it very sharp-edged indeed.

For instance, the greatest happiness principle would license the shooting of hostages or the torture of children, if the result would be for the greater happiness of the greater number. Pontius Pilate has had a terrible press for allowing Jesus to be crucified, although he knew him to be innocent, and hence for putting what was expedient before what was right. But, for a utilitarian, whatever is truly expedient is thereby right. The accent is on 'truly', however, and John Stuart Mill's classic *Utilitarianism* (1861) opens by arguing that the gospels, properly understood, portray Christ as a utilitarian. If Christ's teachings were followed by all, he maintains, the greatest happiness would result. Critics have found this hard to swallow, although it does make the fair point that utilitarian solutions to moral problems need not be brutal or short term. But the principle needs to keep a sharp edge, if it is to be morally distinctive, and that means, for example, being willing to murder an innocent person, if one knows that it will save ten useful lives. Do the gospels really imply that a surgeon should kill a patient in order to transplant the resulting organs into ten others?

The edge is very sharp, if the principle says that each single *action* should produce the greatest (net) happiness. In that case one must always be willing to tell a lie or break a promise and it is hard to see

how utilitarians can ever rely on other people's honesty or trustwor-
thiness. But this snag is at least less obvious, if the principle is put in
the form of telling us to follow the *rules* that produce the greatest
happiness. Since truth-telling and promise-keeping are useful rules,
the utilitarian adopts them and can be trusted after all. Similarly, the
surgeon hesitates, while deciding whether it is for the best to have
all surgeons killing patients to get at their organs. Presumably it is,
however, provided that the truth does not get out and, in general,
since only consequences matter, the best rules recommend the
sharp-edged choices, with a clause about not being found out.
Besides, there is a crucial question of what to do if other people do
not follow the best rules. In an imperfect world, should the maxim
be to tell useful lies and break promises, whenever there is a net gain?

Questions like these lead deep into moral philosophy. Meanwhile
let us assume that there is a coherent version of the greatest happiness
principle to be had and that it gives sharp advice, which conflicts with
an ethic of duty. Now, return for a moment to Mill's claim that
Christ was, in truth, a utilitarian. The abstract point of it is that
actions, even if commended by God, are not good in themselves.
There has to be a reason why they are good (or why God commends
them) and it can only be that they make for greater happiness. Why
is this so? It is, says Mill, because the pursuit of happiness is the only
final motive which people have. (I quoted a famous passage on
pp.28–9). People want all sorts of things but there is always a question
of why they want them. Whatever the reply, the question repeats,
until finally stopped by the answer that they will make someone truly
happy. That is finally why we want health, wealth, company or
anything else.

Gyges' comment will be that the final answer has one further step:
it is finally rational for him to do what will make a particular someone
happy, namely *himself*. Can utilitarianism somehow persuade him
that his interests are so bound up with other people's that this extra
step is in truth a mistake? That will be the opening question of the
next chapter. The idea is to show that, by treating the pursuit of
happiness as a supreme reason for doing one thing rather than

another, we can put Gyges in a position where he has to be guided by the total happiness and not merely by his own. We shall see. In the meantime, there are some threads which need gathering up.

Conclusion

Knowledge of right and wrong is not seen by everyone as a matter of Reason. Indeed, Reason is sometimes denounced as an enemy of sound morals, because it injects doubts where strong convictions are needed. You are welcome to take this view; but it is not mine, because it seems to me that people often do harm out of strong conviction. I ask of ethics that it offer a systematic way of knowing, or at least of having warrant for believing, that a course of action is right or wrong. Both 'Duty' and 'Best Consequences' make the offer and it is interesting to compare them.

Both survive the damage done to traditional moral thinking by the rise of science. The damage is not that moral absolutes have been exploded, since religious faiths continue to flourish. It is that moral beliefs become hard to justify rationally, when science takes over the canon of rationality. An ethic which lays claim to Reason, then, has two tasks. One is to supply the tools for deciding rationally that x, rather than y, is the right thing to do. The other is to show that in doing x a person is acting not only morally but also rationally.

'Duty', in the hands of Kant, attempts the first by analysing the notion of a moral reason. To act morally, I must have a certain sort of reason. I must act on a maxim which is categorical and universal and which will, therefore, not let me treat other people as means to my ends. This test rules out some reasons for action as moral reasons and, if the idea works fully, will let me discover the strongest moral reason in each situation. At the least it stops me exploiting people with a good conscience.

'Best Consequences', in utilitarian hands, offers a sort of calculus (charmingly named 'the felicific calculus') for finding the strongest moral reason. I must work out what will produce the largest amount of happiness, after subtracting any misery caused too. In one version I am to do it on each occasion; in another I am to work out what set of general rules would have this effect and then apply them. (There are other versions too but the overall aim is the same.) Happiness is a matter of what people truly want. The calculation may be difficult but it can be done at least roughly and so as to eliminate some courses of action.

Both approaches thus make it central that a moral point of view is an impersonal one. Duty applies equally to everyone; the happiness of one person counts for the same as anyone else's. Both underwrite the useful test, 'Would I say the same, were I in your position and you in mine?' If I would not, my reasoning is not truly moral. This test is in fact a contentious one, since it tends to suggest not only that I must not favour myself but also that I must not favour my family, friends or compatriots. But there is no denying that there needs to be something to some degree impersonal about a moral point of view.

That is why the second task is difficult for both. It seems clearly not to follow that, because x is the moral thing to do, I would be rational in doing it. Thanks perhaps to the awe inspired by economics, we are very inclined to think that rational action is self-interested action. If so, it will be rational for me to be moral, only when the moral solution benefits me. The fable of Gyges' ring is a graphic way of demanding a warrant for believing that the moral course remains the rational course, even when I lose out. Without that warrant, no ethics will be able to lay a convincing claim to have Reason thoroughly on its side.

Both approaches try to supply it through a theory of human nature and human freedom. Very broadly, the idea is to paint a picture of a fully developed human being, whose talents are fully and satisfyingly deployed and whose character is as he would ideally wish it to be. Self-realization comes from self-knowledge, self-direction and self-discipline. Gyges' life of pleasure and glory lacks a crucial dimension, open only to someone who cultivates the moral point of view. That makes it finally rational to be moral, as Socrates argues in Plato's own reply to the fable of Gyges' ring, which is at the heart of the *Republic*.

The plan can be stated only in very broad terms because there are so many ways of trying to carry it out. Kant's way is a very abstract account of 'the universal concept of a rational being', who turns out to be a moral being, in the sense described earlier. The utilitarian way is more down to earth and relies on a desire for happiness, which is the only final motive of human beings. It depends on showing that we are interdependent, so that the truly free and happy person is one who cares about others as a matter of course. There will be more on these matters in the next chapter.

I may have seemed to imply that every promising theory of ethics must come up with an impersonal, systematic point of view, which makes it rational to be moral. If so, the impression needs correcting. There are many philosophers who do not see ethics as an exercise in distinguishing true moral statements from false ones and who do not believe that one's moral choices should be impersonal. For instance, the special claims of friends or family may be placed at the core of the personal moral life. Love may be seen as a morally transforming experience, which excludes other people at large. There are ethics of commitment or self-creation which do not stop to ask 'What if everyone did likewise?' Although some religions share the concerns of Kant or of utilitarians, others have a very different portrayal of the good life. Many social or political theories have moral concerns which stem from theories of human nature very unlike any so far mentioned. I do not mean to rule out these many and diverse roads to understanding. An invitation to wrestle with some central riddles of recent ethics is not a claim that they alone are worth thinking about.

Meanwhile, the modern world has less magic and mystery than the old. The light of reason beats harshly on beliefs which cannot be rationally defended. How shall moral beliefs withstand the glare?

8

The Common Good

Recent English-speaking philosophy has been prone to conduct its business in the first person singular. Typical questions are: How do I know that a demon is not deceiving me? What does the 'I' of 'I exist' denote? or Why should I be moral? Sometimes the 'I' is just a dummy term, meaning 'anyone' and sometimes it is just a way of inviting the reader to be the dummy. But even in these uses it gestures to a standpoint, which is held to be particular and primary. From here, human knowledge of the world relies on a special access which each person has to their own experience. Knowledge of other minds depends on special knowledge of oneself. A basic job of ethics is to talk each of us out of egoism. For such concerns the *Meditations*, with its duel between the individual and the sceptic, is exactly the right setting.

These remarks are about questions of knowledge and what gives warrant for various sorts of belief. They apply also to questions of what is finally real. Not only in ethics but also in social and political theory, the use of 'I' marks a conviction that the properties of groups are really the properties of individuals who comprise them. Armies exist only because individual soldiers do, national pride is the pride of individual compatriots, political rights are the rights of individuals. There is an analogy with the old belief that everything is composed of atoms, except that the atoms of social life are the carriers of moral significance too.

Individualism is deeply embedded in recent Western thought. But it has never been accepted by everyone and some objections have been noted in earlier chapters. They amount to a refusal to regard 'I' as the basic component of 'we'. For instance, it may be that knowledge requires shared beliefs and public standards or that the self exists only in relation to other people or that it is easier to explain why *I* should be moral, once it is asked why *we* should be. With this last suggestion in mind, let us resume the puzzle of why it is rational to act from moral reasons.

We had got as far as agreeing – at least for purposes of argument – that there is such a thing as the moral point of view but were unable to see why it was rational for Gyges to be guided by it. The moral point of view is impersonally concerned with what is for the best, regardless of who in particular benefits: Gyges is concerned with what benefits himself and does better by not acting impersonally. Since we reached this position both for an ethic of duty and for an ethic of best consequences, it does not matter which we continue with. So let us see what more can be done with a utilitarian approach.

The Social Contract

A fresh line of advance is offered by the idea of resting morality on a notional social contract. If society is composed of individuals each pursuing their own advantage, it can be asked why societies exist at all. A tempting answer is that they arise through a contract which individuals make among themselves for mutual benefit. The contract is freely and rationally made, if each individual gains from it. Gains can be secured, only if all agree to abide by rules of conduct, which bind even on occasions when obedience does not pay. Suitable rules will be marked by the moral point of view, since they will be impersonal in the ways described earlier. A contract freely and rationally made is a moral contract.

The basic social contract could not have been a real event, since contracting can be done only by parties who understand and practise the making of contracts. But the rules of any society are as if agreed by contract, if they would have been accepted by all in advance as the best way of improving on life without them. That sounds tortuous but the basic idea is very neat. For example, Thomas Hobbes set it down memorably in *Leviathan* (1651), arguing from his own picture of human nature. In chapter 13 he addresses 'The Natural Condition of Mankind as Concerning their Felicity and Misery'. The natural condition, he says, is a gloomy one because people are driven by desires which cannot all be satisfied and which lead them to destroy or subdue one another. Since even the weakest has strength enough to kill the strongest, each needs protection against all others. They can count on protection only where there is 'a common power to keep them all in awe'. Without one, 'every man is enemy to everyman'.

> In such condition, there is no place for industry; because the fruit thereof is uncertain; and consequently no culture of this earth; no navigation, nor use of the commodities that may be imported by sea; no commodious building; no instruments of moving, and removing, such things as require much force; no knowledge of the face of the earth; no account of time; no arts; no letters; no society; and which is worst of all, continual fear, and danger of violent death; and the life of man, solitary, poor, nasty, brutish, and short.

These dire facts of human nature give all a mutual interest in creating 'Leviathan', a community with sovereign power over them. On the frontispiece of the original edition Leviathan is portrayed as a crowned king, armed with all the weapons of church and state. Look closer and the king is made up entirely of tiny human beings. That catches the individualist idea of the social contract nicely. Hobbes' version is a fierce one, requiring that Leviathan be given absolute authority, although only for the limited purpose of protecting all and of enforcing any later contracts made in the course of business or social life. That is because of his stark view of natural man and later thinkers have proposed more amiable accounts of human nature, and so of the form which a social contract can take, which need not delay us here. I cite Hobbes, however, for his very revealing analysis of why the contract needs to be binding and enforceable. It is not only because men are by nature enemies (which one might wish to doubt) but also because they are prone to defeat their own interests by acting rationally. Here is a paraphrase of the crucial argument.

Suppose you and I and others are in a business where cooperation pays everyone. Suppose, for instance, that we are whalers and are conducting a free-for-all, which will shortly make whales extinct. There are still enough whales left to give everyone a decent living, while conserving stocks, if everyone limits his catch. No one is fool enough to ease off in isolation but everyone can see the advantages of a treaty. So, it seems, we rationally get together and make a convenant. Furthermore, it seems also, since we all gain, we all rationally keep to it. Where is the problem?

The snag is that in practice we all proceed to break the covenant. (I mean 'in practice': this is a real example and there are plenty of others.) Nor is this because in practice whalers are not rational. On the contrary, we would act rationally in ignoring the treaty, provided only that none of us cares directly about the welfare of other whalers or about whales for whales' sake. In other words, we need not be natural enemies or whale-haters. It comes about because the reasons for making the treaty are also reasons for breaking it. We need a treaty because each of us, left to himself, has an interest in killing as many whales as possible, whatever the others do. Suppose each must decide whether to kill many whales or few (where 'few' is enough for a decent living but 'many' is more profitable). Then each of us has this order of preference for the four possible outcomes (many by self and few by others, few by self and few by others, etc.).

	Self	Others
1st	many	few
2nd	few	few
3rd	many	many
4th	few	many

Each of us, being rational, reasons as follows. If others will kill many, I prefer to kill many (i.e. I prefer 3rd to 4th choice). Equally however, I prefer 1st to 2nd choice: if other whalers are going to be moderate, I shall still do better with a large catch. So it suits me to kill many whales, *whatever others do*. With everyone reasoning like this, the result is everyone's 3rd choice. Everyone takes a large catch and the whale is in danger of extinction.

Since everyone's 2nd choice would clearly be better for all than everyone's 3rd, we make a covenant. But the next question is whether to keep it. If it is only a gentlemen's agreement and we are not gentlemen, we have this list of possibilities:

	Self	*Others*
1st	break	keep
2nd	keep	keep
3rd	break	break
4th	keep	break

By similar reasoning, each finds it better for him to break the agreement *whatever others do*. The only way to stop the conclusion is to make it impossible (or enforceably costly) for anyone to break the agreement. That, in a nutshell, is why Hobbes holds that 'covenants without the sword are but words and of no strength to secure a man at all' and argues that we all need a central power, with a monopoly of force, to keep us all in awe.

The argument has been disputed on the grounds that people are not as selfish as Hobbes says. Certainly, it is not obvious that life in a community without a strong central police force would have to be as nasty, brutish and short as the Wild West (or England in the Civil War, which inspired *Leviathan*). But, to repeat, his case does not depend on a premise that each of us is always trying to get one up on the rest. To see just what it does depend on, let us be more abstract. Suppose each of us has two options, x and y; and suppose that each of us ranks the possible outcome like this:

	Self	*Others*
1st	x	y
2nd	y	y
3rd	x	x
4th	y	x

If others will do x, self chooses x (3rd and 4th lines); and if others will do y, self chooses x (1st and 2nd lines); so self chooses x regardless. The result is x all round, with the 3rd best outcome for all, even though, with y all round, the outcome would have been better for all.

Another practical example is the situation in a drought, when everyone is asked to save water. Everyone would do better if everyone saved water than if no one did. Yet, if each person's best result is that others save water while he uses it, and his worst result is when he alone saves it, then no one saves water. Or think what happens, if a trust-box is placed in a car park, instead of paying an attendant, or everyone is asked politely to 'Keep Britain Tidy' by taking litter home from picnics. There may also be a terrifying example in the arms race, where each peace-loving nation nevertheless stockpiles weapons and fails to agree to or keep to an inspection procedure. In that case, the penalty for choices which sum to everyone's third best outcome could be the destruction of life on earth.

Crucially, by the usual definition of 'rational', each person acts rationally in helping to cut his own throat. That makes it prudent to have a covenant, so that the choice is no longer open. By giving Leviathan a sword, Hobbes makes it prudent also to keep the covenant. Perhaps, however, there is no need for a sword, if people act morally by sticking to their promises. In that case, it pays to be moral, which is what we were trying to prove.

Such an account is more often given for political than for moral obligation, especially when discussing the role of government in a market economy. A free society can flourish on competition among individuals, provided that each makes it his duty to play fair. 'Duty' means that each keeps his bargains as required by the moral point of view, even when it happens not to pay and there is no enforcing sword. Here lie some absorbing complexities of political theory, however, and in mentioning this political version of individualism, I am only planting a marker. But it increases the interest of the idea of contract to notice how it links moral with political philosophy.

Being rational, Gyges can see the usefulness of making covenants. He has all sorts of projects which will succeed only if there is a reliable public moral order. So he can also see the usefulness of everyone else keeping the covenants made. But his ring means that he can get away with breaking them himself and it removes the reason he might otherwise have had for ignoring his own top preferences. So he, at least, will not be impressed by the proof that morality pays. Nor is this just because he has a power of deceit which the rest of us lack. In a small face-to-face community, where people know each other well and are still there tomorrow, when today's deceits come to light, most of us lack the power of the ring. But in a fast-moving urban-style society of strangers we have it. There are a dozen occasions every day when it pays not to do as you would be done by. A solution to the puzzle which does not work for Gyges does not work at all.

Justice and Morality

'Covenants without the sword are but words and of no strength to secure a man at all.' Hobbes says this in part because he deems us as so self-regarding and competitive by nature that we cannot gain the benefits of cooperation by reason alone. It is one thing for each of us to see that we shall all fare better if we all do what is to our mutual advantage, and quite another for anyone to act on this insight. Hence sanctions are needed to prevent free-riding, he argues. An obvious retort is that human nature is not so disagreeable. Do we not have at least a streak of natural sympathy for others, of fellow-feeling in our nature?

This plausible suggestion is made by David Hume. He credits human nature with a mixture of passions, groupable roughly into those to do with 'self-love' (ambition and avarice, for example) and those to do with 'sympathy' (as with generosity and friendship). Granted that our motives thus include the good of other people, it sounds easy to show that we would often act rationally in contributing to the common good. When we want to help one another, we do not need a threat of swords or social disapproval. Interestingly, however, Hume does not believe that our other-regarding passions are enough to solve a problem set by what he terms our 'partiality' towards ourselves. They are directed at people close to us, our nearest and dearest, our friends, neighbours and compatriots. That we are partial to more people than ourselves alone is of some help; but a thorough solution depends on our being *im*partial. Society will work only if we can sometimes be impartial between those we like and those we dislike or between friends, enemies and strangers.

He says this when discussing the rules of justice (and property), which he conceives as dealing impartially between A and B, whoever A and B may be. Justice requires that A keep agreements with B and honour obligations to B, whatever their personal relationship or lack of it. This remains a standard view in recent Western analyses of justice. It is shared by those who disagree about whether justice is essentially a matter of giving everyone their due or of meeting people's needs of respecting their rights or of recognizing their deserts. Whatever the preferred criterion for justice, to act justly is to adopt an impartial, impersonal and universal point of view, reminiscent of the Kantian moral point of view in the last chapter.

Hume describes this impartial standpoint as 'a remedy in the judgement and understanding for what is irregular and incommodious in the affections' and, because our natural affections involve partiality, regards justice as an 'artificial virtue'. This then lands him in trouble, as he confesses gracefully, when it comes to explaining why people are rational to act justly on occasions when it would suit them better not to. In discussing the difficulty, he introduces a 'sensible knave'. This fly character grants that honesty is a good general rule but adds that it is a rule prone to many exceptions and then argues that a person 'conducts himself with most wisdom, who observes the general rule and takes advantage of all the exceptions'. If justice were indeed an artifice aimed at securing mutual benefits, the knave is being entirely sensible and Hume is stumped for a retort, 'if his heart rebel not against such pernicious maxims'. The merits of artifice being a matter for the head, rather than the heart, the knave wins the argument, I fancy.

You could try suggesting here that we do in fact have a natural sense of justice. Small children hardly need to be taught to exclaim 'That's not fair!', when given a smaller share of the cake, and the idea of fair shares can seem innate. But Hume is in good company when he claims that our natural moral sentiments are all biased to us and ours and extend only as far as we can widen our own circle. If he is right to argue that impartial rules are artificial, we shall need a fresh sort of reason for not taking advantage of them, when we can do so without penalty. Hence Hobbes' problem of social and political obligation is not resolved by widening our natural sentiments to include sympathy for other people.

Swords and sanctions ranging from legal penalties to social pressures no doubt help to make us act justly when we could otherwise avoid it. But, if they are not enough to keep sensible knaves – meaning all of us when not actively trying to play fair – in line, what else is there? The answer may finally be a direct appeal to morality, implanted by nature or discerned by intuition. But this would be to abandon hope of reasoning ourselves into believing that it is rational to aim for a common good, even when we could do better for ourselves by acting immorally or unjustly. If an impartial point of view is indeed 'artificial', we cannot appeal to sources of morality and justice prior to social relations and rational deliberation. So, can we find reasons internal to social life for acting as free and willing contributors to the common weal, when the writ of external sanctions fails?

Before we try a final answer, here is a further ground for treating justice as an artificial virtue and the rules of justice as an artificial remedy for what is incommodious in human nature. It concerns the idea of a liberal and tolerant society which upholds moral variety among its members. A liberal society embraces citizens who disagree about the character of the good life and about the sources of legitimate moral authority. With democracies growing more plural, it is becoming both more urgent and harder to state a principle to determine what shall and shall not be tolerated. The basis of any such principle is being ever more strongly challenged by groups with their own ideas of how the good life should be led. Some of them are distinctly illiberal, for instance in their view of women, gays and other ethnic groups, and they claim the right to educate their children into their beliefs and practices.

This sets liberals an urgent problem of finding a basis for citizens' obligations, while respecting conflicting moral views. One familiar line is to distinguish between procedural and substantive values. Procedural values are those of fair play, as embodied in rules of the social game like equality before the law, free speech and freedom of conscience. Substantive values are those which go with specific ideas of the good life, often but not only religious, and which infuse alternative life-styles. The distinction is then often marked as one between justice ('the right') and morality ('the good'), with justice thought of as a neutral between moralities. Thus John Rawls in *Political Liberalism* speaks of a just society as 'a fair system of cooperation between free and equal persons' and sees fairness as a neutral idea, acceptable to people of all moral persuasions.

Yet it is proving a hard task to draw and hold this line. If fairness implies equal access, for example to the process of law, does it also imply a fair share of resources – a good lawyer as well as an open-minded judge? If it implies equality of opportunity, for instance between men and women, then some people reject it on moral grounds. Does equality of opportunity presuppose a good education and a basic income? Does a good education include the lesson that men and women are equal? Does a basic income include the price of holidays and should it be given as of right to those who choose not to work? The more we think about the detail of fair provision for free and equal persons, the more we see that procedural values, even if neutral between some ideas of the good, are still morally charged.

A like point can be made about the neutrality which goes with freedom of conscience, thought and speech, in short the liberal values which justify toleration. The standard idea is that we should be free to think and do as we please and to join with like-minded others for the purpose, provided that we do not harm anyone else. A just society has neutral, procedural rules which guarantee this freedom. But what counts as harm? Physical harm can usually be neutrally defined – for example, assault, theft and the dumping of toxic chemicals in rivers. So perhaps can some kinds of psychological harm, like mental cruelty. But can I harm others by offensive behaviour, for instance by public indecency, incitement to racism or publishing what they regard as blasphemous? A moral note emerges, when liberals reply that it depends not only on whether other people are offended but also on whether they are entitled to be. This reply is usually couched in a language of rights and bound up with a distinction between what is properly to be regarded as public or private. Here again the liberal line, even if neutral in some ways, is still morally charged.

I do not mean to deny all distinction between justice and morality, between procedural and substantive values, between the right and the good. But I do suggest that neutral is not to be read as morally non-committal. Hence, we should not view a society which embodies 'a fair system of cooperation between free and equal persons' as a sort of club for people wanting their backs scratched. There has to be more to a just society than rules of convenience whose only basis is mutual benefit. Otherwise there will be no grounds for complaint when sensible knaves join the club, evade the security system and take advantage of all the exceptions. Liberalism has to remain a fighting creed which deploys moral reasons for toleration, for setting limits to toleration and for defining justice in a way which upholds freedom and equality.

The last two sections are not decisive, however. They block any easy link between individual gain and mutual fair play. But they also call for the reopening of a topic shelved earlier.

Rationality and Freedom

Hume's bout with the sensible knave ends with a parting shot, unconvincing in its context but potent when we think further about freedom. He signs off with the comment that sensible knaves are too smart for their own good, since they are 'in the end the greater dupes, and have sacrificed the invaluable enjoyment of a good character, with themselves at least, for the acquisition of worthless toys and gew-gaws'. I shall try finally to connect the enjoyment of a good character with the idea that knaves in general and Gyges in particular have forfeited a crucial kind of freedom.

Freedom is plausibly taken as the power to do what one wants. We have been assuming that the freedom of the ring is in Gyges' interests and that he is rational to use it. Although we noticed before that it is not always rational to pursue what one wants, we assumed for the time being that it is always rational to act on desires whose achievement will truly give lasting satisfaction. This is the moment to reopen the matter and ask some deeper questions about the freedom which comes with power.

The simplest definition of freedom focuses on a lack of obstacles and sounds innocuous enough. You are free to do something, if nothing prevents you. But that is not very interesting, if freedom is to be a Good Thing, since you are unlikely to care about obstacles on roads which you do not want to use. So let us add a reference to wants. You are free to do what you want, if nothing prevents you. In this spirit, freedom of the seas exists, if mariners can sail where they want without restrictions; a free market is one where people can buy or sell what they please; a free press is a press which can publish what it cares to. Similarly, political, religious or moral freedom can be measured by the degree of restriction on the pursuit of one's own political, religious or moral ends. As Hobbes remarks pithily, 'the liberty of subjects dependeth on the silence of the law'.

As soon as wants are mentioned, however, there is more to say about them. An individual often has wants which cannot all be satisfied and removing an obstacle to one may obstruct another. King Midas' new freedom to indulge his love of gold left him less free to enjoy life at large. For a modern example think of drug addicts who cannot resist the next fix, if they can get it, but can manage a fairly rounded life, if they cannot get it too easily. If they prefer a rounded life, free access does not make them free agents. They are, in an instructive phrase, slaves to their habit. Earlier, perhaps, they had merely failed to foresee the consequences of becoming addicted; and that is another way in which free access may satisfy the desire of the moment without making for freedom in the end. Now, however, what seemed freedom turns out to mean slavery. Obstacles to freedom, in short, can be internal as well as external.

There is thus a tie between being a free person and being a rational person. Desires must be coherent with one another, aided by ordered priorities when they conflict. To be a free agent, you need to know not only what you truly desire but also what is likely to happen if you act on your strongest desire. Given self-knowledge and foresight, you may be rational to welcome external obstacles which stop you doing what you know that you would come to regret. In such cases, having the power to do what you want is not freedom. Notice, however, that no moral judgement is being made here. The point is solely about success. Rational persons are freer because their desires are well ordered by the test of whether achieving them would give true and lasting satisfaction. There is no suggestion (yet) that evil desires are less likely to succeed.

It becomes plainer that obstacles do not always reduce freedom, when we consider groups of people. Your desires may be coherent and mine may be coherent too; but yours may conflict with mine. That is the classic reason for the theory of the social contract again. We can cooperate to mutual benefit, only if there are rules governing what we may and may not do. With conflicting desires, the rules do not let everyone have everything each wants but they give everyone the half a loaf, which is proverbially better than no bread. So a free society is not one without rules and it does not always increase freedom to abolish a restriction. The rules of navigation, for instance, increase the freedom of the seas.

Rules may also help in a more fundamental way. Take the rules of chess. They do not just allow people to do something which they had been wanting to do, as the rules of the sea help frustrated sailors. Before chess was invented, the world was not full of people with a frustrated itch to move knights and bishops. Nor were there knights and bishops waiting to be moved. Chess creates new aims, new desires and new reasons for action. The example is small scale and the game wholly artificial but it will serve for a general and central aspect of social life. Art, religion and science, for instance, may have a touch of a primordial urge but they take specific forms, which emerge only with the rules and institutions which govern them. As with chess, to abolish the rules of the Catholic church would be to abolish the Catholic religion. The making of music has an external purpose but take its internal purposes away – its rules of form and composition, its measures of performance and its rituals – and only noise would be left, if anyone still wanted to make it.

Hobbes' social contract shows how people, who already have desires, can rationally combine to satisfy more of them than they can manage in a state of nature. They cooperate for tactical reasons and their social life together is an instrument to their separate ends. That is why he is sometimes regarded as an early spokesman for the virtues of a free market system, where the market is a useful device for private purposes. The general principle of market freedom is the fewer restrictions the better, although Hobbes has no doubt that some rules, very strongly enforced, are essential. From this angle, the freedom discussed so far is individual freedom, with the rationality needed for it an instrumental rationality.

We get a different story, if we focus on the 'internal' character of the aims and desires which people have in social life. A priest is very unlike a trader. There have been, no doubt, priests, whose heart is not in it and who merely exploit their office for private ends. But consider a priest sincerely committed to the service of God in a ministry defined by his church. His dealings with people are not just tactical. They are the fabric of his ministry and his way of serving God. They are concerned with expressing his faith and with doing good in a manner which needs to be read symbolically as well as instrumentally. He is still a person as well as a priest and has private ends outside his office. But one end, which he has as a person, is to serve God and it may make him critical of some rules of his church. He is not just a puppet. Here we have a notion of a person, which is not the earlier social contract notion (although it occurs in some later versions of the social contract).

The priest's freedom can still be described as a power to do what he wants. But his wants involve a different idea of success, measured in terms of the moral worth both of the outcome and of the means of achieving it. Also there is a further question about his wants, beyond whether they are internally coherent. When he prays to 'God, whose service is perfect freedom', he implies that there are some wants he is freer without. God's service, let us assume, is a tough one and asks what not even a committed priest always wants to do at that moment. Yet, he believes, there is perfect freedom in coming to want what the service demands. Freedom, then, is the power to do what he would *ideally* want to do. With this suggestion, a moral dimension comes into view. Anyone with a priest's beliefs will have a moral idea of what it is rational to do.

It may be misleading to take a priest as the example, since it suggests that this notion of freedom is a nobler one. The same idea could be illustrated, however, by a committed samurai, terrorist or storm-trooper. It is that we can also think of a person internally to social relationships and their meaning, by contrast with an individualist standpoint, and that, when this is done, the concepts of freedom and rationality change. Whether they change for the better is a further question. Meanwhile, we can now contrast the ideas of freedom neatly.

If the test of freedom is simply whether people can do what they want, there are two ways to set them free. One is to remove the obstacles. The other is to change the wants. The first way is what we normally have in mind, when comparing, say, market economies with command economies to see which system gives which sorts of people greater freedom. The other way smacks of dictatorship, as in *Brave New World* (1932) by Aldous Huxley, where the system engineers people with just the wants which it suits the system to satisfy. But, if freedom really is just the power to satisfy wants in a stable and lasting manner, one way produces as free a society as the other. Indeed, *Brave New World* may well be more efficient at preventing unsatisfied desires and, hence, be more free. For, by the test proposed, a happy slave is freer than a frustrated citizen.

To avoid this result, one must insist that there is something amiss with the wants of the happy slave. They are coherent, well ordered, realistic and satisfiable. So why is the slave not free? The answer has to be that there is a test of freedom independent of present wants and their achievement. Curiously, happy slaves are unfree because they could not satisfy wants which they do not have. But this can be taken in two different ways. The simpler merely ascribes a lack of foresight or knowledge. They do not realize, for instance, how bleak old age will be for a slave or how great are the pleasures of the social world beyond their horizon. Their lives are less satisfying than they know. The other reading sets less store by satisfactions. It issues a call to an ideal life and defines freedom as the living of it. It is a risky reading, since it gives an alarming licence to manipulate people's wants. Do those fanatical, irreversible sects and cells truly have the secret of the ideal life? If not, their vaunted freedom is a worse slavery. On the other hand, I do think it crucial to recognize that many existing wants are shaped by existing forms of social life, and to retain a standpoint for criticism. So it makes sense to me to seek a test for picking out the wants essential to freedom.

The most promising moves are, I believe, in terms of rights or of needs. For example, freedom of conscience can be put in either way. If it is a right, which every society ought to recognize, we have a freedom with a moral content at once. If it is a need, which is essential for people's full development as human beings, the moral content is less obtrusive but appears when needs are offered as reasons for treating people in some particular way. Such reasons are moral reasons, even if an ethic of needs is different from one of duty or of best consequences. Either way, Gyges' wants are now open to question and he must be able to defend them, before it is rational for him to satisfy them. He is no longer a free agent merely because he has a ring of power.

The contrast is thus between a 'negative' idea of freedom, which defines freedom as a lack of obstacles, and a 'positive' idea, which sets out the kind of life suited to free agents. The 'positive' idea is the more ambitious and also the harder to make out, witness the wildly different pictures of human nature in a free society, which social, political and religious thinkers have proposed. But even the more modest 'negative' theories have a model of human beings too. It is one of people as seekers of their own happiness, who cooperate freely when it suits them to do so and who act rationally when they do what is likeliest to secure their ends. This is a disputable model and those who uphold it must show it to be a true one.

Even Gyges has a reason to act morally, then, if he cannot otherwise live as he has reason to want to live. The touchstone is the true nature of human beings. If you are content with a 'negative' definition of freedom as the power lastingly to satisfy any set of desires, then the ring remains a welcome improvement on the tiresome work of moral reflection. If your definition is a 'positive' one, then there are no short cuts to a worthwhile life. Since there are, I fear, no short cuts to deciding the right definition, I can only record my vote for the 'positive' side. Here are some concluding reasons.

We noticed at the start that prizes cannot be won by cheating. Cheats do, of course, end up with medals, applause and fine possessions. But they do not have what these goodies symbolize. They have the misplaced respect of other people but misplaced respect also does not signify what it seems and it cannot fool an honest cheat. Of course an honest cheat does not want true respect. The counterfeit is just as useful and self-respect comes from outwit-

ting the people thus fooled. But, all the same, the cheat's relationships with other people are false. Genuine respect cannot be had by
cheating.

Generalize the point to all Gyges' relationships and we find that
the ring has cost him a whole dimension of life. The queen does not
love him for himself, he has no true friends, his subordinates are, in
a subtle way, his slaves. Even in a hierarchical society, the relationships marked by duty require mutual respect and are marked by
moral duty only when the respect is truly grounded. In a society
where people meet, at least in important ways, as equals, the equality
needs to be genuine, if regard is to be moral. That suggests to me that
our fully fledged concept of a person is a moral concept and one
which does not apply in full to Gyges. It requires an honesty for
which there are no short cuts. I still grant that the king's life probably
beat being a shepherd. But it was not all that Gyges might have
wanted and I do not accept that he has fared better than honest
persons could 'at the hands of gods and men'.

At this point we would need to plumb the idea of a good society,
as one where people are free in some 'positive' sense. There is no
shirking the task, granted that the call to an ideal life, without a
demonstration that the life proposed is truly ideal, carries a high risk
of tyranny. Yet Gyges should not be left to win by default. Otherwise
the free life will be the averagely wicked life. Those of us who lack
the power of the ring will be rational not to attempt more than
average wickedness. But we will also do well to avoid the pains of
moral effort, which go with being even averagely good. Instead of
attempting so deep a plunge into social and political theory,
however, let us end with the connection between self-knowledge
and the moral nature of a person.

Conclusion

These last three chapters began with a stout self, which defied
whittling away by the demon of doubt. This 'I' has proved very

elusive. It eludes inspection even by an inner eye. Protected from doubt by not being bodily, it eludes the inference which one mind tries to make about other minds. Not even self-knowledge is infallible, in the face of self-deception or simple ignorance of one's own inner being. There is no pure ghost in the machine. But we are not just machines without ghosts. We are agents and the self is to be seen in action by understanding people's actions. That makes 'I' less individual and private, more public and social, but preserves a special awareness of self which each of us has.

We are, moreover, rational agents and moral agents. Rational agents act with full knowledge of their own desires or interests and of the likely results of their actions. Moral agents have moral reasons. A possible connection is that actions are rational when they are guided by knowledge of right and wrong. But that is easy to attack. Moral truths are, it seems, not known directly not are they known by proof or by evidence; and it is not in the least plain that it is rational to act from principle. So, even granted that there is a moral point of view, impersonal and impartial, why adopt it?

A tempting answer is that people do better for themselves by acting from duty or in pursuit of the general good than they would by doing what suits themselves alone. Although this is not true in quite the terms stated, it invites a fresh look at notions of rationality and self-interest. If the concept of a person is a moral concept which sets a standard for those whose relations with other persons are conducted with integrity, then, after all, it pays to be good. The missing link is a notion of 'positive' freedom, which takes the hunt into a wider social and political theory.

Are we to be good, then, only because it pays? Readers with religious convictions will not be alone in objecting. But my aim has been solely to find a sense in which moral reasons are trumps, which a truly rational person treats as trumps. They are impersonal cards whose value is not measured by personal gain. The schematic argument leaves plenty more for ethics and religion to say about the shape of a good life.

9

Robots, Apes and Angels

What are we? There have been many attempts to say what makes human beings unique in kind. We are self-conscious, rational, creative, moved by sensibility. We can fall in love, jest, write sonnets, extract square roots, plan for tomorrow. We are capable of faith, hope and charity and, for that matter, of envy, hatred and malice. We know truth from error, right from wrong. The list is long and untidy. Some entries seem only a matter of degree. Animals too can hold beliefs, feel and communicate. Machines can extract square roots and organize a complex plan. With nature not fully understood and computing in its infancy, it is rash to pick out any human attribute which is not just a matter of degree.

Yet there has been a persistent belief that we are somehow unique in kind. The best favoured candidate is less specific than any on the rough list above. It is free will. Human actions are chosen; everything else is pre-programmed or happens by chance. Much hangs on the presumption of free choice. It is there whenever we treat people as agents and not as objects, whenever we praise or blame them, whenever we hold them responsible. It is there too in every 'Good morning', 'Thank you', and all the small coins of social life. Even those thinkers who deny free will grant that they will have to rewrite the very language of morals, religion, law, politics and social life at large. If belief in free will turns out to be a complete mistake, the overhaul will need to be radical. Even if the trouble lies only in talk of the *will*, a language which spoke of free action, without ever presupposing free will, would still be disturbingly different from our familiar one. Certainly, the last three chapters would need rewriting.

Almost every sentence about the self, ethics and the common good has added a line to a portrait of us as, however mysteriously, creative beings with choices to make by the exercise of will.

Science has a different angle of vision. It places us in a realm of nature, governed by laws of cause and effect, where everything behaves predictably in given conditions. It points out many ways in which human beings conform. Our bodies obey the laws of physics. We have a chemistry which responds to medicines and influences our thoughts and feelings. Our minds work in ways which biology, computing and the social sciences are learning to account for. Conversely, however, nature – especially human nature – is not simply 'out there' waiting to be investigated. We have repeatedly found that the mind cannot be wholly self-effacing in knowledge. There is active interpretation in our judgements of truth; and science too is creative work, where choices are made in deciding what to believe. The problem of free will is most starkly posed by contrasting ethics, which applies only where there is choice, with science, which applies only where there is not. But it soon emerges that both halves of the contrast reproduce the tension. Ethics requires an orderly world, and science relies on creative intelligence.

So, can we try thinking of human beings in a way which combines free will and causality? The attempt will be better made, if we start with the tension in stark form. Engineering students are periodically given a 'black box' problem, in the form of a sealed box with wires in and out and an attached array of switches and lights. By flipping various sets of switches, they can turn on different combinations of lights. The task is to work out what circuits are in the box without opening it. Think of human nature as a 'black box' problem of a ferocious kind. It is not only that no one can open any other box but also that we are not even transparent enough to ourselves individually to be sure what is in our own. Does each human box contain just very complex wiring or does it contain free will?

The commonest answer is still recognizably Descartes'. There is a self-conscious, rational self inside, who receives information and, aided by memory, emotions, general beliefs and moral principles,

decides on a course of action. The box is thus rather like a signal box
in a railway system and contains a signalman. Information arrives as
input, the signalman chooses the buttons to press or levers to pull,
and messages are sent out to change the lights and switch the points
on the track. A different choice would produce a different output.
The model would not score much in an engineering examination
but here it is (figure 5).

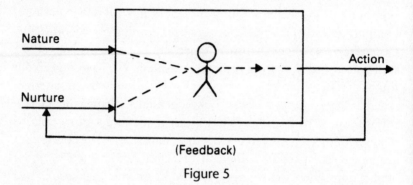

(Feedback)

Figure 5

The matchstick figure does nicely for the 'I' of 'I think, therefore
I am.' 'Nature' refers to genetic endowment and other apparatus
which nature supplies. 'Nurture' is the series of encounters with the
world and other people, which influence each next choice, and the
feedback arrow is a reminder that one's own previous actions have
an influence too. For Descartes' own version, there is a hint that the
rectangle marks the limit of the physical world, with everything
inside it belonging to a mental realm. The dotted lines are dotted to
suggest that they differ somehow from causal linkages, although in
ways not yet clear.

The reference to Descartes is only by way of example. The model
itself is a very general one. The matchstick signalman represents any
variant of the claim that human beings determine their own outputs
and do not merely transmit the effects of their inputs. Equally,
although crucial for ethics, it is a model meant to show what human
beings essentially are. It represents any concept of a person, which

includes free will in the idea that actions are done by persons. It does not even depend on construing the signalman as a substantial self, soul or blob of identity. For instance Jean-Paul Sartre remarks in *Existentialism and Humanism* (1945), 'In life a man commits himself, draws his own portrait, and there is nothing but the portrait.' *Nothing* but the portrait? It is a startling thought and one which whets a curiosity to see what existentialist ethics makes of the idea of moral responsibility. I cite it here, however, just to show that the accent falls on persons as active subjects rather than as spiritual objects.

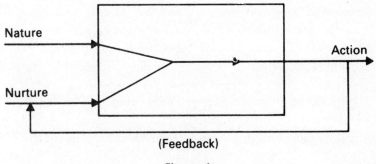

(Feedback)

Figure 6

In the opposing model (figure 6), the black box contains only circuitry or a computer program. Psychology, neurophysiology and various social sciences seem to have fared nicely with this hypothesis. There is much dispute about the proportions of nature and nurture and it can sound as if, since advocates of 'Nurture' usually deny free will, advocates of 'Nature' are upholding it. But that is not really so. The 'Nature' input requires no free will; the genetic code, for instance, is no source of free will. The Nature *vs.* Nurture dispute is more a matter of trying to decide how many of the millions of kilobytes in the human computer are Read Only Memory (ROM) supplied by the maker and how many are Random Access Memory (RAM), for use by upbringing and environment in programming the output. RAM *vs.* ROM is not an argument about free will, even when we add the thought that advanced, complex

computers can be programmed to use their feedback to repro-
gramme themselves.

This model too is a very general one. It represents any version of
the claim that human beings are a subsystem of a system of nature
fully governed by causal laws. How dramatic the claim is depends in
part on how strongly the notion of a causal law is construed. We have
already glimpsed the image of nature as a machine (a watch, for
example), governed by iron laws and forces, which Descartes and
Newton espoused in the seventeenth century. By this reckoning no
subsystem of nature can possibly have the principle of independent
action which free will seems to demand. That is one reason for
Descartes' distinguishing mind from body and insisting that the self
was not part of nature. But the model itself need not be a harshly
mechanical one, since it goes very well with softer accounts of
causality.

One softening, which affects the scope of causal laws rather than
their character, occurred when physics accepted an ultimate element
of chance or indeterminacy in nature. In quantum theory (I am told)
particles retain a finite, if tiny, probability of waywardness. Whether
because they are finally cussed or because observers cannot be wholly
detached from their observations, Nature seems to have an unpredictable streak. In that case it is not an utterly complete system and
some thinkers have tried using the point as an opening for free will.
Whether it truly serves the purpose will be considered presently.

A more significant softening has come with modern, flexible ideas
of cause and effect. The men of experiment (the Ants of chapter 4)
were in search not of iron, necessary laws but of reliable patterns. The
difference is that, whereas what happens in a world of iron laws and
hidden forces *must* happen, events in a pattern are merely regular in
given conditions. That the difference is deep and important was
powerfully argued by David Hume in his *Treatise of Human Nature*
(Book I, Part III). He reasons not just that necessities in nature are
beyond our ken but also that they are not there at all. The world
which we learn about from experience is the sort of world which
experience reveals – one of observable facts and regularities. But

these are all science needs. Science can get along famously with probabilities instead of 100 per cent necessities. Hume's analysis of cause and effect into regular sequences occurring with high probability in given conditions remains contentious. But let us accept it for purposes of argument, to see whether, as has often been claimed, it makes the world safe for free will.

Causality becomes still more flexible with the 'web of belief' theme of chapter 5. If a causal law is barely more than a general statement which we choose to subscribe to, the idea of pre-programmed nature retreats further. If the mind is active, rather than passive, in knowledge, then science itself has a central place for free will. On the other hand, granted that our web of belief is not wholly at our discretion, there are still constraints to reckon with. The traditional puzzle changes character perhaps; but it does not vanish.

At any rate, figures 5 and 6 capture the traditional dispute between 'free will' and 'determinism'. By 'determinism' I mean the proposition that every event has a cause, implying that each event is predictable, given the previous conditions and the laws of nature. That seems also to imply that only one history of the world is possible and hence that human actions cannot deviate from this one path. By 'free will' I mean the proposition that, when human beings do something, they could (at least sometimes) have done otherwise. That seems crucial, if there is to be any moral responsibility for choices made. The traditional tension arises because there is no responsibility without free will, and no free will, if determinism is true.

This is not to commit the social sciences to the side of determinism. Although I have just given social science examples of the circuitry diagram, there are also plenty on the other side. Every social science is divided on the issue. For instance, the core of economics is taken by some to be a study of how economic agents rationally choose to allocate resources and by others as a study of the forces which shape the economy. Some sociologies portray us as creating our social world, whereas others make us its creatures. Some psychologists subscribe fully to a deterministic model and others reject one. Many historians tell a tale of influential, voluntary choices made at critical moments but others see the past as phases and movements, which sweep the actors along. In other words, the truth of determinism is an open question for the social sciences at present and that is one reason why it is so interesting.

'Only What Happens is Possible'

It is also wise to bear in mind that the traditional puzzle is older than the rise of modern science. Admittedly, the tension between free will and determinism became more acute when Nature came to be thought of as a machine, rather than as a purposive, almost organic system. But the trouble has its roots elsewhere. Religious thinkers had long been aware of it. Suppose that there is an all-knowing, all-powerful God, who has created the world and everything in it, including us. Can this God also have given us free will? The mainstream of Christian teaching has always insisted that we have freedom to choose between good and evil. But it has also recognized a problem for this belief, arising because our choices are known to God from the beginning. It is helpful to consider the problem in two steps, by taking 'all-knowing' separately from 'all-powerful', so as to discover just what is troubling for free will in the idea that human actions are predictable. Here is Boethius presenting one side of the argument in a debate from *The Consolations of Philosophy*, written in the sixth century AD:

> If God beholdeth all things and cannot be deceived, then what He foreseeth must inevitably happen. Wherefore if from Eternity He doth foreknow not only the deeds of men but also their counsels and their will, there can be no free will.

That is a tight argument, which makes no reference to God's power. God already knows what you will give your sister for her next year's birthday. When the time comes, you will go through the motions of choosing. Perhaps you will find it a difficult choice. But God knows already what will go into the balance, how you will conduct the weighing and what its outcome will be. Since he has known it from Eternity, another result or even another route to the same result is impossible. Your 'choice' is an illusion and her thanks for it will be out of place. The same is true for all your other actions, for all their causes and for the whole history of the universe which they belong to.

You might try replying that *you* do not start by knowing what you will choose. On the contrary, you are dogged throughout by a strong sense that many gifts are possible and it is this feeling of freedom which constitutes your free will. That is a feeble retort. People often feel free, when they are not. The conjurer's victim feels free to pick any card. Someone, unwittingly locked in a room but not wanting to leave, feels free to leave. People, hypnotized to stand on their heads at a signal and then made to forget the hypnosis, give all sorts of ingenious reasons for what they sincerely think is their own choice to stand on their heads. Free will in such cases is simply an illusion.

Boethius' point can be stated without reference to God at all. Here it is, as proposed in an Ancient Greek book of logic:

If anything happens, then it was going to happen.
Hence it was true before it happened that it would happen.
So only what happens is possible.

This argument can have a curious impact. In order to avoid the conclusion, some people dispute the second line by denying that any statement in the future tense is ever true (or false), since the future does not exist today. That means denying the first line too and leaves one wondering what scientific predictions can possibly be about. Yet is it really true that, if you will choose your sister a book, then you cannot possibly choose her a ball instead? The best answer, I think, is a simple 'No', on the grounds that the conclusion does not follow. From the first two lines it follows merely that only what happens is what happens – not an alarming result.

In that case, an all-knowing God is no more alarming. Your deeds will be what they will be. Your counsels will be what they will be. Anyone who predicted them correctly would speak the truth. All truths are known to God. There is no 'must happens' in any of this and no threat to free will. But now turn to the other attribute of God, omnipotence. If God has engineered the world down to the last detail, then he has engineered our hardware along with everything else and the course of human history is the causal outcome of interactions in the initial state of the system and thereafter. This is a formidable threat, which has led some religious believers, like Calvinists, to accept predestination and dispense with free will. There is the same threat, however, without God at all, if nature is governed by a complete set of laws which allow only one series of states. Omnipotence need not be divine; it is enough that every event be the effect of a previous cause which makes it happen.

It might now look as if all depends on whether there are random elements. If there are, then it is false that the series of events is uniquely determined in advance. There is, then, a way for human actions to be unpredictable. On reflection, however, that is no help whatever. Your free choice of a book for your sister's birthday does not hang on the faint chance that, when she unwraps the parcel, she will find it to contain a rubber duck. You knew she wanted a book, chose one and intended her to have it. A random element would merely interfere with your free will by making your actions less under your control. Random occurrences have no explanation (else they would not be random), whereas choices can usually be explained by saying why they were made.

But, in explaining why a choice was made, we seem also to explain why it could not have been made differently. That is the traditional threat to free will from determinism. The choice has causes, which have causes, which have causes; and so on for ever. Yet responsibility has nothing to do with randomness. There is nothing gained by rejecting determinism and nothing saved by accepting it. Is this the end for free will?

A Neat Solution?

That would be the result, only if determinism truly excludes choice. Otherwise, something different follows – that whether an action is freely done depends not on its being unpredictable but on what sort of explanation it has. Let us next try contrasting free actions not with those which we are caused to do but with those which we are compelled to do. Sometimes you do what you want, sometimes what you must. If you give a beggar money because you are moved by his distress, you have done it freely; if because terrorized by the gun in his hand, you have done it under compulsion. (A calculated response to a threat of 'Your money or your life!' falls in between, as one might expect in what now becomes a matter of degree.) When you sit at a piano, the notes depend on your intentions; at a pianola they depend on the pre-punched holes in the turning scroll. To generalize the examples, all actions have causes, some of which make the agent responsible, while others do not. Any remaining anxiety about causes always compelling their effects can be soothed by accepting Hume's view of causal laws. If there is no necessity or productive force in any sequence of cause and effect, but merely a regularity found in similar conditions, then causes never literally compel their effects. 'Compulsion' is merely a term used when actions do not result from our own wants and intentions.

A neat solution to the problem of free will has suddenly emerged. The problem was posed by dividing actions into two groups, 'free' and 'caused', with the snag that there seem to be no uncaused actions and, in any case, uncaused actions, having no explanation, are not

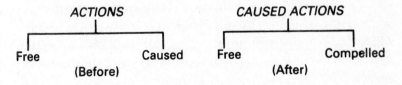

Figure 7

free actions. It vanishes when we recognize that all actions are caused and then subdivide them into 'compelled' and 'free'. Figure 7 is a brisk summary. The issue, it seems, is wrongly stated as free will *vs.* determinism. Indeed we can act freely only in so far as determinism is true. Our free actions need causes, otherwise we would not be responsible for them. This neat conclusion is often taken to show the power of clear-headed philosophical analysis.

Freedom and Reasons

I wish I thought this sewed it all up. Return to 'Your money or your life!' It is not good enough to assign the case to a limbo between pity and terror. If the test is whether you hand the money over because you intended and wanted to, then you hand it over freely. But that does not settle the question of responsibility. Roughly, if you are a bank clerk and the beggar is robbing your bank, you will not be held morally to blame. Yet not everyone always pays up at gunpoint. There are heroes who refuse, especially in other situations, where religion, personal loyalty or political commitment is involved. For instance, soldiers have sometimes preferred to be shot than to obey wicked orders. Such actions are often praised, implying that the agent has made a good choice. So there is an ambiguity about 'compulsion'. You are compelled to do something in one sense, if you could not physically have avoided doing it and, in another, if you could not reasonably have avoided doing it. The first sense squares readily with the idea of a general predictability. The second does not.

What it is reasonable to expect of people depends partly on their situation and partly on their character. It is unreasonable to expect bank clerks to die for their banks but (perhaps) reasonable to expect us to lay down our lives for our friends. It is unreasonable to expect a kleptomaniac to refrain from stealing but reasonable to punish a shoplifter. As far as prediction is concerned, however, these differences are obscure. In principle, it would seem, every action is equally predictable from situation and character. Even kleptomaniacs do what they most want at the time and, presumably, would not steal, if their wants were different. Even heroes would act otherwise, if their characters were otherwise. If 'reasonable to expect' meant merely 'rational to predict', assignments of responsibility would merely reflect the incompleteness of the social sciences (including psychology). But it also means 'entitled to ask' and we do not yet have a basis for being entitled to ask anything.

This is not a moral point but one about the preconditions for moral judgements. Intuitively speaking, shoplifters choose, in that they could have done otherwise, and kleptomaniacs do not choose, since they could not have done otherwise. The bank clerk could have done otherwise and hence, unlike the kleptomaniac, is up for moral assessment. These intuitions are not copper-bottomed but they are intensely plausible and the philosophical analysis claimed to reproduce them. But in fact it does not. In figure 7, the 'After' diagram, it emerges, is not just a neater way of managing what 'Before' muffed. Nor is the difficulty removed by replacing the idea of causal necessity with that of predictable regularity in given circumstances. Something has been lost in the transition from 'Before' to 'After'.

If so, it lies in the difference between choosing and doing. If you choose x over y, then you *could have* done y. The mere doing of x does not have this implication and, on the present account, freely doing x requires only that, if your wants or situation were different, you *would have* done y. In so far as 'could have done otherwise' differs from 'would have done otherwise, if . . .', and choosing implies the former, the very idea of choice has dropped out. With it goes the very idea of free *will*, to be replaced with that of desires satisfied by what happens next. Freedom, in other words, becomes the power to do or get what one wants. The translation leaves no place, however, for agents' choice or control of their own wants by shaping their own character. The final difference between kleptomaniacs and shoplifters is that the latter approve of what they are predictably doing, whereas the former do not.

We can reach this result by a different route, if we recall Signalbox

Man, who, mysteriously, has a will. This seems to mean that he can act differently on separate occasions, even though he has the same beliefs and desires each time. He chooses x, when, without anything else being otherwise, he could choose y. That, on reflection, is very odd. It seems to make his will a random element, rather like spinning a coin. It also seems to leave it inexplicable why he chose x and not y, since there would be exactly the same antecedents whichever he chose. A different outcome would need a difference in what explains it. This line of thought puts a query over the will, which, it suggests, is better regarded simply as the winning desire. Thomas Hobbes, for example, who would subscribe to the 'After' diagram, remarked in *Leviathan*, 'The will is the last appetite in deliberating' and this is just what the diagram implies. Suppose that you are torn between duty and prudence. Duty says 'stay and fight'; prudence says 'run'. Both desires weigh with you but finally one outweighs the other and becomes your 'last appetite'. The process is not quite like an old-fashioned grocer's scales with two pans slung on a crossbar and the heavier pan going down. There is also deliberation. But that too is a process of cause and effect, as with a computer solving a problem. The whole business is one of transmuting input into output by the sort of steps envisaged in a wiring-circuit answer to the black-box question.

That creates the impasse. On the one side, we need to preserve the difference between 'could have done otherwise' and 'would have done otherwise, if . . .'. On the other, it is no good treating the will as a random variable, which intervenes between the winning desire and the action. So let us try locating the agent's control a stage further back. I have just described a conflict between duty and prudence as one between two desires. But that need not be how it appears to the agent, who might well have little *desire* to stay and fight, even though believing that he has a strong *reason* to do so. Indeed prudence is not in itself a desire but a kind of reason for acting on a desire, say, to run away. In that case the agent has a conflict of *reasons*, whose outcome may lead to acting on a weaker desire to fight and so to overriding a stronger desire to run.

A choice between reasons is less like a weighing in the grocer's scales than is a choice between desires. The agent needs to judge which reason is better, whereas the heavier desire simply tips the scales in a mechanical way. The difference shows itself even in simple cases like deciding between jam today and bread tomorrow. Assume that, if only today's desires mattered, you would choose the jam and that your *present* desire for bread tomorrow is not strong. You know that tomorrow you would much regret a choice of jam now. But tomorrow is tomorrow. To make what you judge the better choice, you have to stand back from your present desires. This is the crucial human ability, which the signalbox diagram provides for, and the circuitry diagram does not. Free will is located at the stage of judgement and in the power to act on what one judges the better reason. The remark that deliberation is a process of cause and effect needs withdrawing, in the spirit of what was said about active judgement in scientific knowledge. The mind again requires a power of its own, even if the nature of this power remains obscure.

What finally is the difference between a shoplifter and a klepto-maniac? The former makes a judgement and acts on it, whereas the latter either fails to judge or fails to act on the judgement. But there is more to it, especially if we try to connect riddles of free will to earlier questions about freedom. The shoplifter is moved by reasons of self-interest and that raises the doubts which attended the failure of Gyges to live up to a standard implicit in the concept of a person. I cannot pretend to have a clear final word on the topic and must leave the next move to you. This is an inconclusive end to the hunt, I fear, but the graveyard of ideas is full of solutions. The problem remains very much alive and I am content to leave it so.

Conclusion

In the last few pages I have tried to uphold the traditional posing of the puzzle as one of free will *vs.* determinism against a leading attempt to dissolve the tension. Let me end by restating the underlying paradox, which remains as deep and difficult as ever. I said earlier that there are two ways of thinking about human beings, each excellently supported but together incompatible. That is still so, even if each has turned out to have its troubles. Let us take the determinist model first.

When a black-box problem solves with a circuitry diagram, the solution is general for all similar boxes. Any box with those inputs and outputs will have equivalent wiring inside and all such boxes are interchangeable. They all instance the same broad set of causal laws and respond in the same way in the same conditions. In this sense any two things of the same sort in nature are interchangeable – molecules with similar molecules, molluscs with other molluscs, one ape with another. Of course individual apes are all different but the differences are in principle predictable, given the differences in nature and nurture. Each ape instances a slightly different particular set of causal laws and that is what makes it individual. That is also the sense in which similar machines differ from one another and the robots of the future, if constructed in a straight line of development from current thinking, will still be automata. For all their complexity, they will sum up as further examples of the circuitry diagram. As we have seen, there is much to be said for regarding human beings as the trickiest example of all.

Theories of knowledge which underline the determinist case have been very much part of the rise of science. Standard accounts of Proof and Evidence make good sense in the context of a rationalist ('spiders') or empiricist ('ants') view of what justifies beliefs about the world. Knowledge is acquired by the processing of information; and that is just as it should be, if the knower is a complex system of RAM plus ROM. But what if knowledge involves active judgement and a framework of ideas? I have argued that it does and hence that the 'middle way' ('bees') has something very right about it. Yet the middle way is not just a blend of both the others. It has led us to think in terms of a web of belief and left an awkward final question unanswered about the nature of truth. All is not shipshape on the determinist side.

None the less we have a strong analysis of rational thought, successful in science and turning on notions of explanation by means of causal laws. But we also have a strong belief that moral thinking is different and yet can be rational too. It is different at heart because the signalman model is precisely not a solution to a black-box problem. It rejects the idea that we are supermachines and would rather we were angels than apes. The self is not interchangeable with others of its kind and is more than a particular intersection of general causal laws. People differ not so much in their nature and nurture as in what they make of these inputs; and the inputs do not determine what is made of them. What does? The final answer, enshrined in a belief in free will, is short and mysterious: a person does.

Troubles set in straight away. The self is very elusive, seeing that it was meant to serve as bedrock. We chased it in vain through Descartes' *Meditations* and caught only wavering glimpses of it in the interactions of social life. Nor was it easier to demonstrate that moral thinking can be rational. There were hints that some notions of freedom and of reasons for action go with the robust sort of concept of a person which belief in free will requires. But I cannot pretend that there is a clear picture to set against the rival one.

In calling it 'excellently supported', however, I am not just making a pious gesture. Most of us lead our daily lives with some robust sense of self and take moral decisions in a way monitored by a robust self-respect. These feats are unnumbered arguments for the signalman and they are underwritten in turn by the systematic success of law and religion in ascribing responsibility to individuals. There is also a long and flourishing tradition in the social sciences of trying to interpret and understand human actions, as historians typically do, rather than trying to find their place in a general order of invariable causes and effects. Literature, too, in so far as it illuminates the human condition, weighs in on the side of the angels, if that is still the right name for human beings conceived in an individualist manner.

So the paradox remains. Each half has troubles of its own, which make it tempting to try for a reconciliation with the other, and there are more ways of trying than there has been space for. So I may have restated it too starkly. But a stark form makes it easier to watch the interplay of closed and open questions and extends a stronger invitation to join in. The book began by asking with proper scientific humility whether there is conscious life elsewhere in the universe. It ends, you might say, by asking in what sense there is conscious life even on Earth. But it is not odd that philosophy ends at home. T.S. Eliot sums up in *Little Gidding*:

> We shall not cease from exploration
> And the end of all our exploring
> Will be to arrive where we started
> And know the place for the first time.

Further Reading

If you are a person who likes to approach ideas through their history, philosophy is a marvellous subject. Its great texts are truly evergreen. They pose the grand questions, which we can neither resist nor settle. They do it in sharp, systematic, often practical ways. They offer theories which are still at work in current thinking. But it is hard to get more than the drift of them without a guide. Their context is not ours and needs recapturing, if their assumptions and terms are to make sense. Their arguments are rarely complete and tidy and one needs to know which matter most for the text itself and for its place in the story.

Bertrand Russell's *A History of Western Philosophy* (Allen and Unwin, 1978) was published in 1945 and remains an immensely readable guide. It has more about ancient than modern philosophy and is full of disputable opinions but Russell's mind and prose have an electrifying lucidity. Another readable work is Will Durant's *The Story of Philosophy* (Simon and Schuster, 1961), done in popular style with a very broad brush. For philosophy since the seventh century, A.N. Whitehead's *Science and the Modern World* (Free Press, 1967) is a good scene-setter, as is Basil Willey's *The Seventeenth Century Background* (Routledge and Kegan Paul, 1979). For something fiercer, try Ernst Cassirer *The Philosophy of the Enlightenment* (Princeton University Press, 1951). The twentieth century is well surveyed by John Passmore in *A Hundred Years of Philosophy* (Penguin Books, 1968) and in its sequel, *Recent Philosophers* (Duckworth, 1985), with English contributions surveyed by Geoffrey Warnock in *English Philosophy since 1900* (Greenwood, 2nd edn, 1982). For a larger canvas, try Robert Solomon's *Continental Philosophy* (Oxford University Press, 1988).

---

* I have usually cited recent editions or impressions, paperback where possible, and the dates are therefore not always the original ones.

For particular texts, there is no substitute for reading the originals yourself. The ones on or just under the surface of this Invitation are Plato *The Republic*, Aristotle *The Nichomachean Ethics*, René Descartes *Meditations on First Philosophy* (1641) and *Discourse on the Method* (1637), Thomas Hobbes *Leviathan* (1651), John Locke *An Essay Concerning Human Understanding* (1690), David Hume *A Treatise of Human Nature* (1739) and *Enquiries* (1748, 1751), Jean Jacques Rousseau *The Social Contract* (1762), Immanuel Kant *Foundations of the Metaphysic of Morals* (1785) and *The Critique of Pure Reason* (1781) and John Stuart Mill *Utilitarianism* (1861) and *On Liberty* (1859). These are all to be had in paperback in several editions, usually with an editor's introduction, and are the classic stuff of basic philosophy courses. This is not to say that they are easy reading or that there are not other thinkers of equal worth; but they have all made a crucial contribution and remain standard points of reference.

Guides crowd the library shelves but I mention especially the *Past Masters* series of short, clear commentaries from the Oxford University Press and, while we are at it, the *Modern Masters* series of similar guides to recent thinkers from Fontana Books. Both these series are in paperback and intended for newcomers to their subjects. Also useful and more substantial is the *Arguments of the Philosophers* series published by Routledge and Kegan Paul.

If you prefer to tackle arguments and problems at first hand, Bertrand Russell again springs to mind. He published *The Problems of Philosophy* (Oxford University Press, 1967) in 1912 and it has dated, but no one, I fancy, has managed to upstage it as a brief introduction to philosophical thinking. Of many others, Arthur C. Danto's *What Philosophy Is* (Penguin Books, 1971) does its job notably well. Thomas Nagel, *What Does It All Mean?* (Oxford University Press, 1987) is a brief and useful guide to the main areas. *Philosophy in Practice* (Blackwell, 1996) by Adam Morton is excellent too.

A way to combine an historical with a problems approach is offered by *The Blackwell Companion to Philosophy* (Blackwell, 1996) edited by N. Bunnin and E.P. Tsui-James. *A Modern Introduction To Philosophy*, edited by Paul Edwards and Arthur Pap (Free Press, 1973) consists of well-chosen and well-introduced readings on various central topics. Paul Edwards has also edited the nine-volume *Encyclopedia of Philosophy* (Macmillan, 1967) whose articles by leading professional philosophers are clear, reliable, helpful and much to be recommended. The forthcoming *Routledge*

Encyclopedia of Philosophy, edited by E. Craig, will be helpful too. Of many dictionaries, I especially recommend Robert Audi's *The Cambridge Dictionary of Philosophy* (Cambridge University Press, 1995).

History and problems also come together in some recent books, which might be called classic. The name which obtrudes is Ludwig Wittgenstein. His *Tractatus Logico-Philosophicus* (Routledge and Kegan Paul, 1975) of 1921 and his later *Philosophical Investigations* (Basil Blackwell, 1953 and, in English only, 1963), which reverses the *Tractatus*, are certainly both classic but I do not suggest tackling them at an early stage without a guide, for instance Anthony Kenny's *Wittgenstein* (Penguin Books, 1973). Much more accessible, although not as durable, are A.J. Ayers *Language, Truth and Logic* (Penguin Books, 1971), which brought Logical Positivism to England in 1936 with panache and a conviction that it settled all problems; and Gilbert Ryle's *The Concept of Mind* (Penguin Books, 1970), designed, as we noted in chapter 6, to dispose of 'the ghost in the machine'.

As we reach the present, I shall leave you to find the very recent books which are likeliest to last for yourself. Here instead are a few reading notes on the topics of the earlier chapters.

Chapter 2 Reasoning

The mechanics of proof and evidence call for a clear, reliable introduction to logic. Of several, Irving M. Copi *Introduction to Logic* (9th edn, Collier-Macmillan, 1994) is well tried and attested. W. Hodges *Logic* (Penguin Books, 1977) and R.C. Jeffrey *Formal Logic* (2nd edn, McGraw Hill, 1981) are good formal primers. For less formal reasoning, try M. Salmon *Introduction to Logic and Critical Thinking* (Harcourt Brace, 1984) or A. Fisher *The Logic of Real Arguments* (Cambridge University Press, 1988). For the source of the diagram (figure 4) see Lipsey's *Introduction to Positive Economics* (Weidenfeld and Nicolson, 1989). Lipsey's *Introduction* itself has a useful introduction; and the message is more sharply stated in Milton Friedman's essay 'The Methodology of Positive Economics' in *Essays in Positive Economics* (University of Chicago Press, 1953). Karl Popper's 'Conjectures and Refutations', in his book of essays collected under that title (Routledge and Kegan Paul, 1969) is crucial for this chapter and the connection with the next three chapters.

Chapter 3 The Cave

Plato's *Republic* is quoted in H.D.P. Lee's translation (Penguin Books,

1955) and *Phaedo*, recording the death of Socrates, can most readily be found in *The Last Days of Socrates* translated by H. Tredennick (Penguin Books, 1954). A.J. Ayer analyses knowledge into 'justified, true belief' very clearly in *The Problem of Knowledge* (Penguin Books, 1956) and his *Foundations of Empirical Knowledge* (Macmillan, 1964) gives a renowned defence of empiricism. The themes from Descartes here and later are sharply analysed by Bernard Williams in *Descartes: The Project of Pure Enquiry* (Penguin Books, 1978).

This chapter and the next two are a preface to epistemology, where a guide would be useful. Try the relevant chapter in *The Blackwell Companion to Philosophy*; or Alec Fisher and Nicholas Everitt *Modern Epistemology* (McGraw Hill, 1995). This is also a good moment to mention the *Oxford Readings in Philosophy* paperback series of readings on various subjects with introductions, published by Oxford University Press. It includes *Knowledge and Belief*, edited by A. Phillips Griffiths.

Chapter 4 *Ants, Spiders and Bees*
Bruce Aune's *Rationalism, Empiricism and Pragmatism* (Random House, 1970) will be found helpful, especially as an introduction to pragmatism, the latest upholder of the 'middle way'. Chapter 2 of W.H. Walsh's *Reason and Experience* (Oxford University Press, 1947) is instructive. Books I and II of *An Essay Concerning Human Understanding* by John Locke and Book I of David Hume's *A Treatise of Human Nature* are crucial, if you wish to pursue the theme. In particular, Hume on causation (Book I, Part III) is essential for the study of that topic. J. Cottingham *Rationalism* is a good guide to the Spiders of the title. The challenge to the 'foundations' argument is most sharply put by W.v.O. Quine in 'Two Dogmas of Empiricism' (in his *From a Logical Point of View*, Harvard University Press, 1953), which is the source of the quotation from Quine in chapter 5. Meanwhile Rom Harré *The Philosophies of Science* (Oxford University Press, 1972) is a lucid and lively guide for this chapter and the next.

Chapter 5 *The Web of Belief*
There is an introductory book of this title by Quine and J.S. Ullian (Random House, 2nd edn, 1978), which I warmly recommend. Thereafter, matters become very intricate and it may be best to pursue them through the recent philosophy of science. Thomas Kuhn, *The Structure of Scientific Revolutions* (2nd edn, University of Chicago Press, 1970) is central,

followed by I. Lakatos, *The Methodology of Scientific Research Programmes* (Cambridge University Press, 1978) and P. Feyerabend, *Against Method* (New Left Books, 1975). A.F. Chalmers, *What is this Thing called Science?* (2nd edn, Open University Press, 1982) is helpful in charting these difficult waters. Ian Hacking's volume *Scientific Revolutions* in the *Oxford Readings* series is useful.

The 'challenging objection' to Descartes' view of experience and language was prompted by Wittgenstein's *Philosophical Investigations*. For a quick, sympathetic guide to the point, see the start of Peter Winch, *The Idea of a Social Science* (Routledge and Kegan Paul, 1968), which I shall cite again when we reach chapter 9.

Chapter 6 The Elusive 'I'
Descartes is again to the fore, with Ryle and Wittgenstein in unfriendly pursuit. Jerome Shaffer's *The Philosophy of Mind* (Prentice-Hall, 1968) is a good general guide. So is *The Philosophy of Mind* by P. Smith and O. Jones (Cambridge University Press, 1986). Keith Campbell's *Body and Mind* (University of Notre Dame Press, 1980) is a crisp start on that aspect of the problem. Brave readers will be interested by chapter 3 of P.F. Strawson's *Individuals* (Methuen, 1964), whose Kantian reflections remain central to current discussion. For a 'Fantasia and Reflections on Self and Soul' (to quote its subtitle) you would probably enjoy D. Dennett and A. Hofstadter's *The Mind's I* (Harvester, 1981). The Other Minds problem soon ramifies, as will be seen from Don Locke's *Myself and Others* (Oxford University Press, 1968).

L.H. Davies *Theory of Action* (Prentice-Hall, 1979) is helpful. Of a large and growing literature on action, I especially like L.W. Beck's *The Actor and the Spectator* (Yale University Press, 1975), which suits the theme at the chapter's end. Jonathan Glover has edited the volume on *The Philosophy of Mind* in the *Oxford Readings* series, and A.R. White the one on *The Philosophy of Action*.

Chapter 7 The Ring of Gyges
There are references for Plato, Hume, Kant and Mill in the text.

For a useful tour of ethics, I recommend *A Companion to Ethics* (Blackwell, 1991), edited by Peter Singer. Bernard Williams' *Morality* (Cambridge University Press, 1976) is short and sharp, or you might prefer John Hospers' stout college textbook on ethics, *Human Conduct* (Harcourt

Brace, 1972). J. Mackie's *Inventing Right and Wrong* (Penguin Books, 1977) is notably clear. D.D. Raphael's *Moral Philosophy* (Oxford University Press, 1981) is an introduction addressed to the theme in the chapter about Kantian *vs.* utilitarian ideas of morality. The idea of 'the moral point of view' is explained by Kurt Baier in his book of that title (Cornell University Press, 1958). The merits of utilitarianism are roundly debated by J.J. Smart and Bernard Williams in *Utilitarianism: For and Against* (Cambridge University Press, 1973). Jonathan Glover applies utilitarianism interestingly in *Causing Death and Saving Lives* (Penguin, 1977), as does P. Singer in *Practical Ethics* (Cambridge University Press, 1993). Bernard Williams pursues the objections in *Ethics and the Limits of Philosophy* (Fontana Books, 1985).

Useful professional essays can be found in Phillipa Foot's *Oxford Readings* volume, *Theories of Ethics*.

Chapter 8 The Common Good

The first mention of the idea of social contract is in Plato's *Republic* Book II, just before the Gyges story. Its main classic theorists are Hobbes, Locke in the *Second Treatise on Civil Government* and Rousseau in *The Social Contract*. Rousseau was much in my mind, when discussing 'positive freedom'. For a general introduction to political philosophy see W. Kymlicka's *Contemporary Political Philosophy* (Oxford University Press, 1990). Questions of the common good straddle ethics and politics and have lately been enlivened by John Rawls's revival of the idea of contract in *A Theory of Justice* (Oxford University Press, 1973) and *Political Liberalism* (Columbia University Press, 1993), although I suggest reading Kymlicka before tackling these formidable books. Two good recent anthologies are *Liberals and Communitarians* (Blackwell, 1992) edited by S. Marshall and A. Swift, and *Communitarianism and Individualism* (Oxford University Press, 1992) edited by S. Avinieri and A. De-Shalit.

Chapter 9 Robots, Apes and Angels

Jennifer Trusted's *Free Will and Responsibility* (Oxford University Press, 1984) is a good starting point, as is D.J. O'Connor's *Free Will* (Anchor Books, 1971). Aristotle's view of responsibility is in Part III of his *Nichomachean Ethics* and his discussion of whether what happens must happen is in chapter 9 of *De Interpretatione*. There are eminent attempts at reconciling free will and determinism in Hobbes (briefly in *Leviathan* chapter XXI, at greater length in 'Of Liberty and Necessity' in *Body,*

Mind and Citizen, edited by R.S. Peters, Collier Books, 1962), in Locke's *Essay* (Book II, chapter 2, section 21), in Hume's *Treatise* (Book I, Part III) and J.S. Mill's *A System of Logic* (Book VI, chapter 2). A.J. Ayer puts an especially clear and neat case in 'Freedom and Necessity' in his *Philosophical Essays* (Macmillan, 1954).

Gary Watson's *Free Will* volume in the *Oxford Readings* series is useful. See especially H. Frankfurt, 'Freedom of the Will and the Concept of a Person' and P.F. Strawson, 'Freedom and Resentment'. Both essays offer subtle ways of involving free will with the concept of a person, which lead on interestingly from themes in the chapter.

Index